THE TALENT ASSESSMENT AND DEVELOPMENT POCKET TOOL KIT

THE TALENT
ASSESSMENT
AND
DEVELOPMENT
POCKET TOOL KIT

How to Get the Most
Out of Your Best People

BRENDA HAMPEL AND **ANNE BRUCE**

Mc
Graw
Hill
Education

NEW YORK   CHICAGO   SAN FRANCISCO   ATHENS

LONDON   MADRID   MEXICO CITY   MILAN

NEW DELHI   SINGAPORE   SYDNEY   TORONTO

1 2 3 4 5 6 7 8 9 0   DOC/DOC   1 2 0 9 8 7 6 5 4

ISBN: 978-0-07-184044-6
MHID: 0-07-184044-3

e-ISBN: 978-0-07-184100-9
e-MHID: 0-07-184100-8

Design by Mauna Eichner and Lee Fukui

Library of Congress Cataloging-in-Publication Data

Hampel, Brenda.
  Talent assessment and development pocket tool kit : how to get the most out of your best people / by Brenda Hampel and Anne Bruce. — 1 Edition.
      pages cm
  ISBN 978-0-07-184044-6 (alk. paper) — ISBN 0-07-184044-3 (alk. paper) 1. Employees—Coaching of. 2. Employees—Rating of. 3. Ability. 4. Employee motivation. 5. Personnel management. I. Bruce, Anne, 1952- II. Title.
  HF5549.5.C53H35 2014
  658.3'12—dc23

                                                              2014013519

Contents

Acknowledgments

Thanks from Brenda Hampel

As I began to outline this book and decided to reach out to colleagues to talk about this important topic, I wasn't sure how everyone would respond to the "invitation." I was pleasantly surprised when each person I asked enthusiastically accepted my request that they talk with me and be a part of this work. I thank each of them for taking the time out of their extremely busy schedules and for contributing their own experiences and successes in the quest to improve the professional lives of the employees they each support and the organizations of which they are a part.

In addition, I would like to thank my dad, Bill Laubenthal. He was the first entrepreneur and leader to introduce me to and teach me the lessons of business. Dad taught me the importance of having a strong work ethic and the value of creating strong relationships with your customers. "Always have a firm handshake, look them in the eye, and smile." These are the words of advice that still come to mind when I interact with business associates. Thank you, Dad, for giving me the foundation I needed to be successful!

And of course I owe a huge thank you to my husband, Jeff, who has the ability to put things in perspective when they feel out of whack and for always believing in me, even when I have doubts.

Thanks from Anne Bruce

It is with pleasure and great appreciation that I acknowledge the people who support my work and make a significant difference in my life and, therefore, in the lives of those who buy my books, attend my seminars and training workshops, and help keep all that I do relevant.

A very special thank you goes to my McGraw-Hill family, my esteemed publisher for 18 years. Thank you to the amazing executive editor and publisher in charge of this series, Mary Glenn, and to talented senior editor Knox Huston. I've done my best to absorb your guidance and wisdom as I've traveled the long and winding road of my publishing career. Thanks for being patient colleagues and friends all these years. A special shout-out goes to our superstar editing and design team: editing liaison Scott Kurtz, Alice Manning, Cheryl Ringer, Mauna Eichner, and Lee Fukui. Thanks, Mauna, for always being available for all the late-night and weekend telephone conversations during the postproduction of this book.

A big thank you goes to my friend and coauthor, Brenda Hampel. As the series' acquisition editor for this book, for me you make all the hard work in today's world of human resources and leadership look attractive, engaging, and special. It's always a pleasure to work alongside you, and I look forward to many more collaborations.

If there were a Pocket Tool Kit book titled *Amazing Friends and Family*, I'd be the author. I am truly blessed and want to say thank you to just a few of my longtime and devoted supporters: mentor and longtime friend, literary agent and executive editor, Mark Morrow, dearest friend on the planet Kim Lehner, "sister-friend," Garrett Speakers International President, Betty Garrett, dynamic duo, best friend and goddaughter, Maureen and Katie McKissick, all of the amazing and talented people at MedAmerica Billing Services, Inc. and their superstar Educational Development Center, where we'll soon get to try out training curriculum from this book, Fired Up! teammates extraordinaire Anmarie Miller, Aric Bostick, and Jeni Croxford, talented novelist and writer DL Winter, awesome and devoted friends Keri Badach, Linda Swindling, Traci and Casey Van Attenhoven, "fascinating" leadership coach Barbara Fagan and everyone at SourcePoint Training, Diana Damron, Dolly Hinshaw, team gurus and "adopted brothers" Lawrence Polsky and Antoine Gerschel, photographer Jamie Koorndyk, who shot the photo for this book, my dear friend and superstar editor Phyllis Jask, best friends Carole and Harris Herman, Diane Panvelle and Glenda Thomas, wonderful "Nonni" Karen Dilallo, my loving sister Rose Marie Trammell, my off-the-charts talented and very special cousin Jeanine Finelli, and many others (too many to list here—but you know who you are). Thank you for your never-ending support and for your unconditional friendship and love.

Finally, my heartfelt appreciation and love go to my loving husband David (20 books later you are still singing my praises), I love you. To my beautiful and brilliant daughter, Autumn, son-in-law Andy, my super-adorable grandson, Nikolai (you are the love of my life), and to my granddaughter, whom I have yet to meet as of this writing, but you are due to arrive soon, aka "Baby Anniversary." I dedicate this book to you, my sweet grandchildren. Thanks for making me the happiest "Grandma Fun" ever!

I love my family and friends more than I can fully express within these pages. All you have done for me has allowed me to write and speak for a living and hopefully make a small but important difference in people's lives around the world. Because of you, I get to live my passion.

THE TALENT ASSESSMENT AND DEVELOPMENT

POCKET TOOL KIT

Introduction

If you're an HR professional, manager, supervisor, or anyone who wants to grow and nurture talent, then this *Talent Assessment and Development Pocket Tool Kit* is your go-to guide. Included in this Pocket Tool Kit are case studies, charts, guidelines, and valuable takeaways that we believe help to promote individual growth and learning, as well as personal and professional development in a workplace that is filled with tough challenges. This book is user-friendly and passes what we call "the flip test." Just flip through, find what works for your team, and give it a try!

Many of us work in a world in which identifying the right talent at the right time can often be tough. In fact, it can be downright exhausting. Yes, there are more challenges than ever for today's HR professional and organizational leadership, but the key is how you equip yourself to keep moving forward and handle the unique challenges you face that will separate you from the herd.

We are excited to be authors in this Pocket Tool Kit series for McGraw-Hill because we understand that bite-size chunks of powerful information, like the ones featured in this book, can help to move both you and your employees forward in a positive and evolving direction. This talent assessment and employee development tool kit is just one piece of a bigger puzzle. We encourage you to read other books in this series that will assist you in building movement and momentum in a breakneck-speed world that requires us to find and identify great talent, attract and hire that talent, nurture those individuals, and then bring their best to the surface. Assessing the best of the best from the start is what this book is all about.

As the authors of this book, we also see ourselves as field guides. Think of us as your virtual coaches and share with us how you actually use this book and how you adapt, delete, or modify its content to suit your specific organization's culture and your one-of-a-kind leadership style. We welcome your feedback and suggestions at any time. We're here to coach and support you in the process.

Lighten Up! Make the Process Fun!

We suggest to you that effective talent assessment and people development starts with turbocharging your environment. So lighten up and make it fun! Whenever possible, hire for attitude and train for skill. Whether you work in a cubicle, on a farm, or in a glass and chrome office tower, attitude is everything! Our message to you is to think of yourself as a talent scout and an excavator of special skill sets and amazing human potential. Be positive! It's time to ignite passion and activate potential, wherever you work and whatever the culture of your business. It all starts with investing in your people. As one adage goes: **What happens if we invest in our people and then they leave us? The reply is: What happens if we don't invest in our people and they decide to stay?** We are confident that this Pocket Tool Kit is a worthwhile investment!

Company leaders can no longer rely on the same old traditional HR practices, career counseling, or business-as-usual career guidance that we once used. All of us have to stay current and do our best to keep up with cutting-edge practices, such as "mindfulness in the workplace" (see Chapter 2 for more on this). It's all about growing mindful, stronger, smarter, more capable, and self-reliant talent that will take your organization into the future and to the next level of success. More than technology, this is truly the most critical issue facing our workforce, domestic and global—talent assessment and ongoing people development. So buckle up and get ready to launch this talent assessment and development tool in your company, department, or division today.

It's time to bring out the best in your employees. We're here to help as your virtual coaches as you continue to use this field guide to identify and assess top talent, and to nurture and grow those around you and those yet to join your organization.

Enjoy this go-to pocket resource and let us know how you're using it in your organization. Remember, within the word *career* is the word *care*.

Your talent assessment and people development coaches,

BRENDA HAMPEL
bhampel@connectthedotsconsulting.com
and
ANNE BRUCE
Anne@AnneBruce.com

CHAPTER 1

Back to Basics

A leader's ability to lead and manage others begins with the ability to lead and manage oneself.

—Unknown

What Is Talent Management?

Wikipedia says, "Talent management refers to the anticipation of required human capital for an organization and the planning to meet those needs. The field increased in popularity after McKinsey's 1997 research[1] and the 2001 book on *The War for Talent*.[2] Talent management in this context does not refer to the management of entertainers." Instead, it refers to the management of the real workers and professionals who make your organization successful.

Wishful Thinking and Hope Are Not Strategies

Again from Wikipedia, "Talent management is the science of using strategic human resource philosophies, processes and practices to improve business value and to make it possible for companies and organizations to reach their goals. Everything done to recruit, retain, develop, reward and make people perform forms a part of talent management as well as strategic workforce planning. A talent-management strategy needs to link to business strategy to make sense." Wishful thinking and hope are not strategies.

Johnni Beckel, chief human resources officer at Ohio-Health (a family of 28,000 associates, physicians and volunteers, 17 hospitals, more than 50 outpatient locations, health and surgery centers, home-health providers, medical equipment and health service suppliers throughout a 47-county area), uses the following mental model to guide her and her team's talent management strategy: Get the Right Talent; Know Our Talent; Grow Our Talent; Move Our Talent which drives our culture and desired behaviors, grounded in our Core Values. Beckel's model reinforces the importance of having a consistent approach that can be applied in any organization. The model also begins with understanding who you have on your team before you determine how to grow it and move them. In her first 60 days in her role at Ohio-Health, Beckel met with many leaders across the organization one-on-one and asked questions to help her understand the culture, the talent, and the ability of the talent to deliver against the business strategy of the organization. By listening and learning during her first months on the job, Beckel built the knowledge base that she and her team needed before proposing, changing, or implementing talent management initiatives. Based on this input, she immediately tested a talent review process for a critical group of nursing leadership, then prepared to expand the process throughout the organization.

The definition given here and the mental model shared by Beckel provide the perfect framework for our approach in this book. If you and/or your organization are defining and applying talent management in a different way, perhaps your first step should be to redefine what talent management is and how you apply that definition.

It is important that you try to understand all the components of talent management. The model in Figure 1.1 provides a broader view of the employee talent management cycle.

Now that we are working from a common definition of talent management, it's time to take an inventory of your talent management function and assess the effect of the function relative to the needs of your organization.

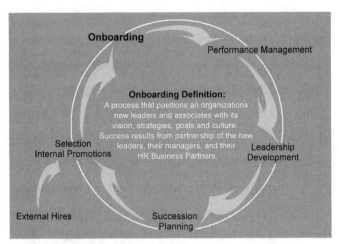

Figure 1.1 **Talent Management Cycle**

Talent Management Inventory

What roles play a part in your talent management function? What responsibilities does each player have? A best-practice talent management (TM) organization includes:

- Talent acquisition

- Onboarding

- Assessment and development

- Performance management

In larger organizations, these responsibilities may be carried out by separate departments. In medium-size and smaller organizations, they may be combined into one or a few departments. Regardless, it is critical that there are clear definitions for each, as well as ownership of the deliverables for each.

Roles and Responsibility Inventory

Use Table 1.1 to outline your organization's current roles and the responsibilities that those in each of those roles have with regard to delivering talent management to your employee population. Table 1.2 is an example of what a completed chart looks like.

Table 1.1 **Organizational Roles and Responsibilities**			
Area of Responsibility	**Ownership**	**Key Deliverables**	**Gaps**
Talent acquisition			
Onboarding			
Assessment			
Development			
Performance management			

Table 1.2 Completed Organizational Roles and Responsibilities Example

Area of Responsibility	Ownership	Key Deliverables	Gaps
Talent acquisition	Director of talent acquisition	• Acquisition strategy • Effective partnerships with external and internal recruitment professionals • Effective acquisition process • Fill positions with the "right" talent within agreed-upon time frames • Strong relationships with hiring managers	Turnover percentage for two key positions is too high
Onboarding	Director, organizational development Human resources business partners	• Best-practice onboarding program and experience that mirrors the organization's business needs and culture • Measurement against objectives	Lack of consistent handoff from acquisition to OD
Assessment	Director, organizational development Human resources business partners	• Develop and execute an assessment strategy • Establish and manage internal and external partnerships that support the strategy • Measure the impact and effectiveness of the strategy	Talent review process is not connected to other key components of the talent management function

Table 1.2 **Completed Organizational Roles and Responsibilities Example** (continued)			
Area of Responsibility	**Ownership**	**Key Deliverables**	**Gaps**
Development	Director, organizational development Business leaders	• Design and implement a development strategy and programs that support the current needs of the organization and engage the employee populations • Measure the outcomes of the strategy against objectives	Lack of an actionable measurement of leadership development programs
Performance management	Director, organizational development Human resources business partners Business leaders	Design a performance management system and process that are aligned with the performance and behaviors needed to drive organizational objectives	

Audit Findings—Mind the Gaps

What did you learn about your talent management function from conducting this simple audit?

- Were you able to complete each section of the audit?

- What gaps did you find?

- What is the impact of those gaps?

- What are your next steps for addressing your findings?

Table 1.3 lists strategies for addressing audit findings.

Table 1.3 **Strategies for Addressing Audit Findings**				
Area of Responsibility	**Ownership**	**Key Deliverables**	**Gaps**	**Strategies**
Talent acquisition	Director of talent acquisition	• Acquisition strategy • Effective partnerships with external and internal recruitment professionals • Effective acquisition process • Fill positions with the "right" talent within agreed-upon time frames • Strong relationships with hiring managers	Turnover percentage for two key positions is too high	• Analyze the following: • Exit interview data • Current candidate sources • Hiring manager input • Partner with hiring managers to identify changes needed to address the gap • Measure the effect of changes

| Table 1.3 **Strategies for Addressing Audit Findings** *(continued)* | | | | |
Area of Responsibility	Ownership	Key Deliverables	Gaps	Strategies
Onboarding	Director, organizational development Human resources business partners	• Best-practice onboarding program and experience that mirrors the organization's business needs and culture • Measurement against objectives	Lack of consistent handoff from acquisition to OD	• Summarize the effect of the gap • Work with OD, HRBPs, and talent acquisition partners to review current practices and identify changes that would address the gap • Agree to the changes • Monitor progress
Assessment	Director, organizational development Human resources business partners Business leaders	• Develop and execute an assessment strategy • Establish and manage internal and external partnerships that support the strategy • Measure the impact and effectiveness of the strategy	Talent review process is not connected to other key components of the talent management function	• Review the outcomes of the current talent review process • What is done with the data that come out of the reviews? • Work with stakeholders to identify opportunities to link talent review outcomes to talent acquisition and development strategies

(continues)

Table 1.3 **Strategies for Addressing Audit Findings** *(continued)*

Area of Responsibility	Ownership	Key Deliverables	Gaps	Strategies
Development	Director, organizational development	• Design and implement a development strategy and programs that support the current needs of the organization and engage the employee populations • Measure the outcomes of the strategy against objectives	Lack of actionable measurement of leadership development programs	• Work with HRBPs and operational leaders to identify the core objectives of the leadership development programs • Develop methods such as brief surveys for both the program participants and their managers that provide input on the effectiveness of the programs
Performance management	Director, organizational development Human resources business partners	Design a performance management system and process that are aligned with the performance and behaviors needed to drive organizational objectives		

The inventory audit expands into an assessment of your talent management practices. The results of the audit and the assessment are invaluable to both the talent management team and the leaders and employees who participate in these practices.

Assessment and Development Focus

Our focus is on the assessment and development components of the talent management cycle. So let's take a closer look at how to assess what you are offering to the organization and the effects of those offerings by conducting an audit.

Your audit needs to encompass a complete inventory of the assessment and development programs and initiatives. It doesn't have to be complicated—a simple chart like the one shown in Table 1.4 can show your offerings and their impact.

Table 1.4 **Talent Management Assessment Tool**			
Current Offering	**Audience(s)**	**Impact**	**Next Steps**
Examples			
Leadership development program	Managers and directors	• 65% of audience attends • Unsure of impact on participants' ability to lead their teams and deliver results	• Review curriculum • Integrate experiential components into program • Add postprogram activities to increase retention and application *(continues)*

Table 1.4 **Talent Management Assessment Tool** (continued)			
Current Offering	**Audience(s)**	**Impact**	**Next Steps**
Examples			
Sales training	New sales reps	• 100% of audience attends • 85% retention of reps in first year • 75% of reps achieve or exceed sales objectives	• Add sales manager module to build managers' ability to coach those reps who are underperforming, and to address the 15% turnover

If you are unsure of the impact of your current programs, or if leaders provide different responses to the question concerning the effects, it is time to assess the work you are offering. A key outcome is the ability to present a business overview and case for either continued support for current offerings and/or for new initiatives.

By conducting an audit, you will learn a great deal, including:

- A full inventory of your practices and how they are, or are not, being used

- An evaluation of the value of your current practices and programs

- An understanding of the audiences served and those that may be under- or overserved

- An understanding of the capacity, competency, and commitment of your talent management resource

- A clear view of the strengths and gaps of your strategy and programs

Next Steps

In order to sell your plan to executive management, you'll need to outline your findings carefully and present solutions for the areas that are lacking. Prepare an executive briefing of your findings that includes:

- Executive summary

- Recommendations for an updated assessment and development strategy

- The business case to support the recommendations

Talent Management Development Plan

Once you have presented your recommendations and gained leadership support for moving forward, leveraging a well-known tool, the development plan, will give you a road map for implementing your initiatives.

An effective development plan includes the following:

Objectives

What are you trying to achieve with your assessment and development program and practices?

Strengths

Identify your strengths. Based on your evaluation, what are the strengths of your program and practices? Do your strengths help you achieve your objectives? Having a leading-edge intern program is effective only if your organization's strategy includes a commitment to grow talent. If the strategy is to "buy" talent to support short-term growth, an investment in an intern program may be an identifiable use of resources, but it is not an actual strength.

However, if you have a strong onboarding program that successfully integrates experienced hires, you are supporting a key organizational objective.

Gaps

What gaps did your evaluation bring to the surface? Remember, it is critical that your program and practices support your business objectives. There may be several gaps on your list; however, you now need to prioritize them based on your objectives.

For example:

- Sales training for a new product

- Business acumen for field leaders

- Successfully managing a multicultural and multigenerational workforce

- Leaders as coaches

- E-learning opportunities

Which will have the most impact on your organization? Use the questions in Table 1.5 to look at each program and determine which will best support critical objectives and deliver a timely return on investment.

What does this evaluation tell you about the program? Should you move forward? Why or why not?

Conduct this evaluation for each gap that came to the surface to help you prioritize your plan by program, timing, and budget to support your organization's objectives. The results will provide you with the most business-relevant gaps and a business case to present to leadership. Table 1.6 shows what a completed chart might look like.

Table 1.5 **Questions to Determine Critical Objectives**

Program	Business Acumen for Field Leaders
Why is this program needed?	
What does success look like?	
What resources, internal or external, are needed to develop and implement it?	
Estimated costs	
Estimated time frame for development and implementation	
Return on investment estimate	
Other	

Table 1.6 **Completed Questions to Determine Critical Objectives Example**

Program	Business Acumen for Field Leaders
Why is this program needed?	Critical to eliminate a key gap and barrier to achieving sales objectives
What does success look like?	• Field leaders have the ability to review business results and apply them to their operational and talent decisions and actions • Increase sales and retention and decrease inconsistent operational practices
What resources, internal or external, are needed to develop and implement it?	• Internal: human resources talent and employee development and coaching; external: curriculum design partner • Time for field leaders to participate in the program
Estimated costs	$350,000
Estimated time frame for development and implementation	9 months
Return on investment estimate	$1.5 million after 18 months
Other	

Barriers

After completing the assessment and agreeing on the top priorities, it is important to identify and anticipate any barriers to success.

Barriers come in all shapes, sizes, and colors. You may not be able to foresee all of them ahead of time; however, the more you can get in front of them, the more likely you are to be able to address and remove the barriers.

The sidebar on retail giant Lane Bryant illustrates the importance and outcome of anticipating and addressing barriers.

CASE STUDY

Specialty Retail—Lane Bryant

Lane Bryant, a leading specialty retailer, conducted a thorough analysis of the skills that sales leaders need if they are to drive both the culture and the sales results needed to reach the firm's aggressive growth objectives. Current sales leaders were then assessed against the success profile. The assessment brought to the surface a clear business acumen skill gap. Human resources and field operational

(continues)

leaders agreed that addressing this gap was critical for long-term success.

The strong partnership between human resources and field operations facilitated a balanced approach to the firm's needs and the appropriate solution. Additionally, the partners agreed that they needed to address a barrier in the form of the number of initiatives that field leaders were implementing in a 12-month period.

In response to this challenge, the HR and field operations teams took two actions. The first was to schedule the training sessions carefully, and the second was to incorporate as many experiential, on-the-job components as possible into the curriculum in order to build business acumen.

By taking the time to identify potential barriers to success and apply strategies to overcome those barriers, the Lane Bryant team executed a successful development initiative.

Measure the Impact

Although many human resources professionals struggle with how to measure the return on investment and the effect of assessment and development programs, others have found both quantitative and qualitative ways to measure them.

Why is it important to measure the results even if no one is asking for them? As a talent management professional, you should measure the impact and effectiveness of your initiatives. Your organization spends financial and human resources on these initiatives in addition to talent management resources.

So how do you measure impact and effectiveness? There are several methods and approaches. The first step is to review your objectives: What do you need or intend to achieve?

Let's look again at the Lane Bryant sidebar and examine the development objectives and business relevance.

Development objective: Equip managers with the skills to manage a multigenerational workforce more effectively.

Business relevance: Review the business case for including this initiative in the development curriculum. The initial evaluation brought the challenge that leaders were facing to the surface: managers were struggling with a diverse employee population made up of baby boomers, generation Xers, and millennials. The leaders found that their traditional management tools were not effective, given the dynamic created by this multigenerational team. Consequences include disengaged team members and silos created within the team. In addition, this type of team situation may lead to employee relations challenges that bring the risk of legal situations.

These data provide the human resources and operational leaders with the outcomes that need to be measured. Here's a way to determine the effect.

Identify the Baseline

QUANTITATIVE

- In the past 12 months, we have seen a __ percent increase in employee relations issues between team members from different generational groups.

QUALITATIVE

- Managers are frustrated by their lack of ability to deal with a diverse team.

- Team members are less engaged.

Track Progress

- Monitor the same data points after the development initiative.

QUANTITATIVE

- The rate of employee relations issues between team members from different generational groups decreased or increased __ percent (or had not changed) six months after the leaders completed the multigenerational training.

QUALITATIVE

- Managers have the skills and tools to address employee relationship issues that arise between team members from different generations.

In Summary

1. Know what you need to measure from the beginning.

2. Identify a baseline.

3. Include both qualitative and quantitative data.

An additional benefit is the demonstration of how powerful the partnership among the organizational development, human resources, and operational leadership can be!

TIPS AND TAKEAWAYS FROM THIS CHAPTER

- Clearly define the talent management players and their roles.

- Study your stat sheets to understand your current state.

- Make adjustments based on your results and what you need to achieve.

- Keep an eye on your scoreboard using quantitative and qualitative results.

CHAPTER 2

Culture:
The Secret Sauce

We want to understand what works here
rather than what worked at any other
organization.

—LASZLO BOCK, GOOGLE

The power and effect of organizational culture are often talked about, but culture is rarely harnessed and leveraged to meet an organization's objectives. There has been an increase in both research and work focused on effectively creating and sustaining winning cultures. A case in point is Adam Bryant's *Quick and Nimble*,[1] in which he observed that several CEOs indicated that they wanted to either create or maintain a "start-up-like" culture, meaning a culture that is able to respond quickly to market shifts, customer demands, and employee expectations in a positive and dynamic way. Leaders who have been part of a start-up culture often refer to it as their best professional experience. They also notice a loss of that culture once the organization matures and becomes more complex. To ward off a slower and cumbersome culture, several CEOs identified and recommend six key strategies outlined in Bryant's book.

Wikipedia's definition of corporate culture says:

Organizational culture is the behavior of humans who are part of an organization and the meanings that the people react to their actions. Culture includes the organization values, visions, norms, working language, systems, symbols, beliefs, and habits. It is also the pattern of such collective behaviors and assumptions that are taught to new organizational members as a way of perceiving, and even thinking and feeling. Organizational culture affects the way people and groups interact with each other, with clients, and with stakeholders.

Each organization has a unique culture and several subcultures. Your assessment and development strategy and practices need to be aligned with and reflect your culture.

When this does not happen, organizations typically struggle with how to engage with and apply programs—they just don't fit. Even if supporting culture change through development is a core objective, this must be done in a way that reflects today's organizational culture and provides a bridge to the desired culture.

As we interviewed each professional for this book, their responses reflected the culture of the organization of which they are a part. For example, a human resources business partner at an off-priced retailer referred to the unique business model that is at the core of his organization's merchant development programs. Cindy Silver, Director of Organization & Leadership Effectiveness at The Ohio State University, embeds evidence-based development into the solutions that she and her team develop for leaders in the organization.

How do you articulate an organization's culture? You often know what it is, but can you put it into words and apply those words to a development strategy? Although it can be difficult to describe an organizational culture accurately, it is possible to do so. An entire industry has emerged over the past 15 years that offers tools and services specifically designed to bring to the surface, articulate, and measure a company's culture. Each of these offerings has a unique methodology; however, they are all striving to achieve the same outcome for their clients. If your organization has data from one of these services, your job is straightforward. Read and analyze the data through the lens of a talent management professional. These data should then be integrated into the assessment and development strategy.

If your organization does not have culture data, the culture audit in Table 2.1 will enable you to ask the right questions to bring to the surface the behaviors and norms that make your organization unique.

Table 2.1 Culture Audit Questions

The following set of questions is designed for a focus group or interview setting. This allows for more discussion and interaction, as well as richer input. It is critical to have an experienced and respected facilitator leading the discussion.

1. How would you describe this company as if you were describing a person (three words)? When you talk about where you work, what do you tell people?

2. What does the company value? What is important here? How do you know it's important?

3. What areas are dominant here—does marketing lead, or is it sales or service? Why?

4. What are the "unwritten rules" for getting along in this organization? What do we always do? What do we never do?

5. How does the organization handle conflict? Good news? Bad news? Deadlines? Decision making? Can you give us examples of ways in which the company has handled crises?

6. If I were a fly on the wall at a typical management meeting, what would I see (process, dynamics, interaction, style)? Would this differ at all if the top leaders were (or were not) present?

7. Describe the process for effectively "selling" an idea here. (How can you influence the decision-making process?)

8. Who do you see as the primary customers of your company? What happens here when a key customer complains? To what extent does the company hold true to its expressed standards for dealing with its customers? Its shareholders? Its employees?

9. Think about a new employee who has been successful here. What has he or she done that has been particularly successful? What is the "success profile" for a new employee?

10. Can you give us some examples of situations where a new employee's onboarding hasn't gone well? Here we're looking for a situation where someone either has left the organization or has managed to regroup and salvage the situation.

11. What advice do you have for new employees?

Outcomes of the focus groups and interviews are analyzed and summarized into a culture road map (see Table 2.2) that articulates behaviors representing the organizational culture.

Table 2.2 Sample Culture Road Map

Over the years, our organization has developed an informal set of "rules of the road." These organizational norms are largely implicit, rather than explicit—you will typically not discover what they are until you have done something outside of the norm. We thought you might find them helpful as you make your transition into our organization.

At Our Company, We Always ...	At Our Company, We Never ...
• Deliver	• Say, "I can't"
• Are flexible	• Say, "This is the way we've always done it"
• Are constructive ("I can")	• Try to cover up
• Look for opportunities to innovate	• Create negative surprises—never surprise leaders, coworkers, or customers
• Are honest (but not brutal)	• Wait for perfection
• Are accountable for mistakes	
• Do something (make a decision)	• Take a media call directly *(continues)*

Table 2.2 **Sample Culture Road Map** *(continued)*	
At Our Company, We Always . . .	At Our Company, We Never . . .
• Keep the right people informed and involved (keep the audience in mind) • Think of things • Communicate—there's a business reason • Focus on customer service • Stay on top of things • Assume that resources are scarce—don't assume that you can give work to a staff of people • Are flexible with your roles and responsibilities • Have a sense of humor	• Disclose financial information externally • Tarnish the company by sacrificing customer service • Are unresponsive (especially to customers) • Assume that our roles will stay the same • Accept or decline a job because of who our manager would be • Say, "That's not my job!" • Take all the credit • Pull rank—we are all accountable to one another

Ask the People Who Know

Who should you ask to gather the information that you need if you are to outline the organization's culture?

It's important that you be deliberate as you identify a sample of your employee population to talk with about the culture. Ask the following questions to assemble the right group:

- How many employees make up a representative sample of your population?

- What divisions, business units, and locations need to be included?

- Do you want to bring to the surface the culture within specific levels of the organization, such as the executive leadership population? If so, we recommend that you gather 10 percent of your leaders for the culture discussion.

What's Your Communication Plan?

Once the decision is made to have a discussion about culture, it is important to build a communication plan. Conversations about culture can be challenging and even emotional. A thoughtful communication plan increases the chances of reaching the intended objectives and outcomes.

Use these questions as a guide to building an effective way to communicate during the culture work:

- What is your message? Having a carefully crafted and authentic message is critical.

- Who should be the author of the message?

- How will focus group participants be invited?

- What will be done with the information that is gathered?

Designing the right message is core to the success of a culture audit and its effect.

The Culture Connection

So what does an organization's culture have to do with its assessment and development work? Everything!

As we noted in the Introduction, when development initiatives are not consistent with the culture, those initiatives miss the mark. There are several consequences, including wasted resources, loss of credibility, and employees failing to receive development resources.

To make the connection, begin by being honest about your current culture. Although driving culture change may be an objective of the development strategy, it is critical that you meet the organization where it is before attempting to build on it. Table 2.3 lists a few examples.

Table 2.3 **Organizational Culture Types and Appropriate Development Strategy Examples**	
Type of Culture	**Consistent Development Strategy**
Mature Finance-driven Large size	• A blend of traditional and innovative programs • Connect to core traditions and norms • Demonstrate the effect of innovation
Start-up Marketing-driven Small size	• Focus on on-the-job opportunities • Leverage the top leadership team • Demonstrate a direct link to short-term objectives

Type of Culture	Consistent Development Strategy
Table 2.3 Organizational Culture Types and Appropriate Development Strategy Examples *(continued)*	
Turnaround Sales-driven Medium size	• "Go to them" delivery of development • Highly focused on short-term impact • Integrate long-term focus
Highly successful Manufacturing-driven Medium size	• Opportunity to introduce new initiatives • Leverage success profile • Build the ability to grow internal talent
High-growth Creative-driven Large size	• Focus on what makes the organization unique • Support the skills needed to support the growth • Balance core functions with support functions; both are critical

CASE STUDY

Retail at Holiday

As talent management and leadership at an off-price retailer began to plan for the upcoming holiday season, they discussed the development opportunities that the critical holiday season often presents. The decision was made to be more purposeful about these opportunities by calling them out ahead of time and setting them up as learning opportunities for field employees. Talent management leaders scheduled a planning session during a time that was historically off-limits for any activity that is not

(continues)

directly related to holiday sales. The return on this investment of time and resources was invaluable!

As a growth organization, this retailer understands
that its growth targets will not be achieved without the
right talent with the right skills and abilities. This requires
the company to be creative and take advantage of opportunities that come only once each year.

CASE STUDY

OhioHealth

Johnni Beckel, chief human resources officer at Ohio-
Health, talked with us about how her organization pro-
tects the unique culture it has cultivated as it has grown.
OhioHealth recently acquired another healthcare organization. Although it was clear to the executive team that the
acquired organization was a strong fit with OhioHealth's
business strategy, it was equally critical to understand and
address any cultural differences. To accomplish this, Beckel
and her team led an initiative to ensure cultural alignment
that included:

- Discussions with executive leadership of the newly acquired organiztion to understand the culture, operating routines (how work gets done) and its goals and objectives.

- A culture assessment of the new organization which included both a formal survey and informal observations

- A side-by-side comparison of the outcomes to the OhioHealth culture

- Facilitated discussions to both clearly articulate OhioHealth's cultural norms and to identify strategies for changing behaviors, practices and organizational systems to help assure success for the newly acquired organization.

Beckel and her leadership team clearly understood that it's the people and the culture that make or break mergers and acquisitions. It is important not to leave culture to chance. With that understanding, they committed time and resources to get in front of dynamics that can get in the way of success. This is truly an example of walking the talk.

Integrating the current culture into the assessment and development strategy and programs enables leaders and employees to understand its value.

Give People What They Need and They May Give You What You Want

Brenda and Anne had the opportunity to speak with Dawa Tarchin Phillips, president and CEO of Empowerment Holdings, to talk about some of his expertise and insights on mindfulness and its effect on organizational culture. Anne visited Dawa in his Santa Barbara offices to find out more about how his leadership development and consulting firm provides mindfulness-based leadership training and professional skills and interventions worldwide.

In my meetings with professionals around the globe, it's no surprise that I've seen people who climb quickly and work diligently because they are smart, well trained, and motivated to be and do their best. What disturbed me, though, was the universal evidence of system resistance, burnout, and ongoing struggles with job satisfaction and work-life balance.

After work, these talented and sincere individuals get together and thrive in collegial, relaxed atmospheres, and when they are allowed to be themselves, they are inquisitive, natural, and authentic, and are inspired to follow what feels genuinely right and true, and is good for them.

If happy hours tell tales, how people behave after work is an indication of how they want to feel while on the job. It is safe to say that they would choose to be emotionally balanced rather than in distress and depleted; they would prefer ample autonomy over rigid, old-world authority; and they would receive rewards for their efforts in the form of genuine well-being, meaning, connection, and fulfillment.

Seeing the Forest for the Trees

What can HR professionals learn from observing what people do privately to improve their life satisfaction—the one thing most negatively associated with voluntary turnover and retention failure?

How can they use growing scientific understanding of what really works for people in order to recruit, retain, develop, and reward people and help them perform at their best?

(continues)

Needn't a cutting-edge understanding of the human mind and body be part of successful talent management as well as intelligent strategic workforce planning?

If the so-called war on talent fails to acknowledge a growing desire for the psychological paycheck, peace, and quality of life among the educated, insightful, skilled, and increasingly independent workforce, ignoring what their best talent wants and needs could come at a significant cost.

Recruitment professionals know too well that recruiting and retaining good people isn't a cakewalk. Replacing newly departed workers can be expensive when the time and costs of recruiting, hiring, and training are considered.

Well-designed assessments and programs targeted at enhancing workers' job and life satisfaction—thus increasing the retention rate—not only are cost-effective alternatives to frequently replacing valuable talent, but could play a bigger role in strengthening an organization's vision, culture, and productivity.

Research shows that the things that work to improve people's overall life satisfaction, reduce stress, and increase their sense of personal and professional balance are ever more affordable and simple to integrate.

They do not consist of elaborate benefit packages, extra pay for overtime, or large year-end bonuses. What people seek out when they are faced with the inevitable need to recenter and balance, access their inherent unlimited creativity, and thrive is a return to simplicity: openness, relaxation, and basic human presence. In short, mindfulness.

In America alone, 10 million people currently practice some form of mindfulness or meditation. Overall, 20 million practice yoga regularly, and the trend is increasing, as are trends in the cultivation of active focus skills and emotional intelligence.

Looking at these trends—mindfulness in particular—what could HR professionals offer in terms of assessment and development that could not only align with what matters and catches the attention of their workforce, but also create an organizational culture not unlike what people are already striving to create in their personal lives?

Aligning the intrinsic motivational drivers of the workforce with outcome measures and professional development can truly unleash the power of each employee into the greater organizational objective.

(continues)

Some, Like Google, Are Doing It

Google's Search Inside Yourself program is an example of how one company engages in assessment and program development that is relevant for the professional performance of its employees and also for the overall well-being and life skills portfolio of its workers. More than 1,000 employees have completed the program; it has a long waiting list, and the success rate is growing.

Conducting relevant and interest-aligned assessments can show new and loyal employees alike that a healthy organizational culture can align with their capacity to be their authentic best while they are at work—for many of them, possibly for the first time in their lives.

Mindfulness-based interventions boost overall life satisfaction, mood, self-esteem, self-confidence, empathy, and resilience in people. So why not in your people? Could assessing mindfulness ultimately tie in to a candidate's skills, abilities, aptitude, attitude, values, and behaviors that your organization needs? I believe so.

To expand your current retention efforts while also giving a nod to intelligent recruitment, consider the roles that mindfulness, basic human presence, and empathy can play in socializing new workers to your organizational culture. After all, these are crucial elements of strong engagement and overall job satisfaction.

Modern trends like "just-in-time hiring and firing"—trends that foster the idea that companies can stay nimble, hire just as a need arises, and lay off workers immediately when business encounters slowing growth—also point to the value of recruiting with mindfulness in mind. Adaptability, openness, and calm readiness for the unexpected are all characteristics that are shown to increase with mindfulness training.

If you're ready to explore forming language and action steps around these concepts, follow these guidelines:

- *Cultivate mindfulness every day.* Do this consciously and by choice. Like compounding interest, it will pay you back handsomely over time. The value and benefit of five minutes of practice today grows exponentially, and will pay you back multifold over a year, five years, or a lifetime. Here is how to start:

  - *Sit or stand in an upright posture.* Find a comfortable seat or posture that allows you to have a straight spine, which quickly translates into
  (continues)

greater mental clarity and allows you to stay alert longer without becoming drowsy or dull.

- *Connect with your physical sensations.* Whether you are walking, standing, sitting, or lying down, connect with your physical sensations in the present moment. This not only grounds you, but also strengthens your empathy because the awareness of your own physical sensations helps you relate more to those around you.

- *Cultivate trust.* Nothing distracts and clouds the mind like ongoing worry and anxiety. Choose to cultivate trust instead. Invest in your ability to be human and simply do your best; don't pursue delusions of grandeur, deny your own vulnerability, or hate yourself for your own human imperfections.

- *"Anchor" your attention.* Focus on your breath, your sensations, or simply a spot on the wall; anchor your attention in the present moment for minutes at a time by returning again and again to the object of your training.

- *Cultivate nonjudgment.* Also called openness or acceptance, this is the decision and ability to suspend self-judgment on your own present mental and emotional state. Shift your focus to fully being with your own state, as it is.

- *Cultivate kindness.* Kindness can be summarized as a commitment to not abusing yourself or others for the sake of money, image, or status, but to engage in big-picture thinking that sees your own well-being aligned with that of those around you.

Next, use the Mindfulness Attention Awareness Scale that follows to begin to assess your organization's mindfulness levels. Should you find your organization lacking, then it's time to reach out to one of the many qualified coaches and consultants who can help your organization tap into this critical ingredient for success and well-being.

Mindfulness Attention Awareness Scale

Using the 1–6 scale that follows, please indicate how often you currently have each experience. Please answer according to what *really reflects* your experience rather than what you *think* your experience should be.

1	2	3	4	5	6
Almost Always	Very Frequently	Somewhat Frequently	Somewhat Infrequently	Very Infrequently	Almost Never

I could be experiencing some emotion and not be conscious of it until some time later	1	2	3	4	5	6

(continues)

1 Almost Always	2 Very Frequently	3 Somewhat Frequently	4 Somewhat Infrequently	5 Very Infrequently		6 Almost Never

I break or spill things because of carelessness, not paying attention, or thinking of something else	1	2	3	4	5	6
I find it difficult to stay focused on what's happening in the present	1	2	3	4	5	6
I tend to walk quickly to get where I'm going without paying attention to what I experience along the way	1	2	3	4	5	6
I tend not to notice feelings of physical tension or discomfort until they really grab my attention	1	2	3	4	5	6
I forget a person's name almost as soon as I've been told it for the first time	1	2	3	4	5	6
It seems as if I am "running on automatic," without much awareness of what I'm doing	1	2	3	4	5	6
I rush through activities without being really attentive to them	1	2	3	4	5	6
I get so focused on the goal I want to achieve that I lose touch with what I'm doing right now to get there	1	2	3	4	5	6
I do jobs or tasks automatically, without being aware of what I'm doing	1	2	3	4	5	6
I find myself listening to someone with one ear and doing something else at the same time	1	2	3	4	5	6
I drive places on "automatic pilot" and then wonder why I went there	1	2	3	4	5	6
I find myself being preoccupied with the future or the past	1	2	3	4	5	6
I find myself doing things without paying attention	1	2	3	4	5	6
I snack without being aware that I'm eating	1	2	3	4	5	6

You just might discover that behind every primped résumé, firm handshake, and bright smile is a person who is ready for a different work experience—one that is engaging, personal, meaningful, and rewarding. And you're the one who can give it to him or her.

Dawa Tarchin Phillips is also a research specialist at the Department of Psychological and Brain Sciences at UC Santa Barbara and the founder and executive director of the Institute of Compassionate Awareness. For seminars, workshops, and keynote speeches, contact Dawa at dtp@empowermentholdings.com or 805-680-3988 or visit www.empowermentholdings.com.

TIPS AND TAKEAWAYS FROM THIS CHAPTER

- Understand the importance of culture.

- Ask the right questions of the right people to bring today's culture to the surface.

- Develop a thoughtful communication plan.

- Make the connection between the culture and development.

CHAPTER 3

The Coaching Staff: Who Is Doing What and When?

I think the most important thing about coaching is that you have to have a sense of confidence about what you're doing.

—PHIL JACKSON

Now that we have laid the foundation for assessment and development work, it is time to focus on the roles and responsibilities of the coaching staff. Who does what and when?

Depending on the size and structure of your organization, the roles may look a bit different; however, the coaching staff is typically made up of the leaders and managers of the human resources business partner (HRBP), organizational and talent management specialists, and senior leadership. Let's start with the HRBP.

The HR function is the key organizational function that usually owns the assessment and development strategy and program(s). In many organizations, there are several departments within the HR function, such as recruitment, compensation and benefits, training and development, employee relations, and so on. Over the past 10 years, the title HRBP has become very popular in all types of organizations. Unfortunately, this title has been overused, and as a result the role has been diluted compared to its original intent. Often the HRBP is the linchpin of an effective assessment and development program.

The HRBP role was created based on the research and work conducted by David Ulrich, a highly regarded human resources professor at the Ross School of Business at the University of Michigan. His book *Human Resources Champions*[1] introduced us to the term *HRBP*. According to Ulrich's definition, the purpose of the role was to be a true partner to the operations and administrative functions (see Figure 3.1).

Figure 3.1

Business Partner = Strategic Partner + Administrative Expert + Employee Champion + Change Agent

This equation illustrates the complexity of the HRBP role. Where do assessment and development fit into this role? As we outlined in Chapter 1, the assessment and development strategy and program must support the needs of the business, and the HRBP best understands the needs of all parts of the business that he or she supports, *and* partners with the assessment and development professionals who will design the programs.

Wear the Right Hat for the Right Task

The HRBP also plays a critical role in the resulting implementation strategy, supports its success, and realizes the effects and return on investment (ROI) of the program. Because the HRBP is such a critical role, let's take a deeper dive into this role and its success profile. Regardless of whether your organization uses this title, the role is essential for successful assessment and development strategies and programs.

Let's begin with the term *partnership*: "a relationship between individuals or groups that is characterized by mutual cooperation and responsibility, as for the achievement of a specified shared goal."

To illustrate the different components of the HRBP role, we have created a three-level module in Table 3.1 that clearly outlines the different competencies needed to be successful. The model further defines the equation that we introduced in Figure 3.1.

Table 3.1 **HRBP Competencies for Success**		
HR Capabilities	**Business Capabilities**	**Consulting Capabilities**
• Employee relations • Gets the basics right • HR subject-matter expertise • Use of HR metrics	• Commercial awareness • Business acumen • Customer focus • Aligning business and HR strategy	• Brokering • Trusted advisor • Impact and influence • Facilitation and coaching • Leadership • Project delivery

The model is based on work conducted by Deloitte Consulting and published in its 2011 report titled *Global Business Driven HR Transformation*.[2] The work articulates the three distinct levels of capabilities needed to be a successful business partner. Let's discuss the importance and teachability of each.

Master Your Business Capabilities

This is often the most challenging area; however, it doesn't need to be. How can you support the finance, sales, or information technology functions if you do not understand the business and how it operates? You probably can't! Make the time to learn about the departments in your organization and take the time to get to know the strengths and challenges of the personnel in them.

Be a Businessperson with Expertise in Human Resources

One of the best compliments I ever received came when I was in the role of HRBP: "You are not a typical HR person; you are a businessperson with expertise in human resources." This gave me the credibility to partner with the leaders and their teams that I supported. So, how did I go about this?

I had a genuine interest in the business. Having or developing a true interest in the business in which your organization is operating makes it much easier for someone to stay informed and knowledgeable. A curiosity about how the organization works, the competitive landscape, and external influences—such as legislation, market trends, and technology positions HRBPs to ask questions and to read and explore the business landscape; this allows them to participate in operational discussions, increasing their ability to support the business and its development needs.

Know Your Business

Here is a checklist of what it would be good to know about your business:

- Its vision, mission, core values, and direction

- Its business model

- The organizational structure of all business units, divisions, and functions.

- Market distinctiveness

- The competitive landscape

- Performance measures for outcomes and ultimate success

Having an understanding of this type of information puts you on a level playing field with your client colleagues and allows you to not only have business discussions but also have a much deeper reservoir from which you can draw in making decisions and developing possible strategies.

How do you gather this information?

- The company website

- Press releases

- Internal meetings and presentations

- Business publications, such as the *Wall Street Journal, Fortune, Fast Company*, and *Wired*, and online resources, such as the *Huffington Post* and blogs and other online resources

- Mentors and internal and external customers

- Specialty groups on LinkedIn or other social media that are focused on your industry's needs

When was the last time you visited your company's website? Most of us rarely do. This resource contains a wealth of information about your organization, and although it is designed for the outside world, those within your organization can benefit greatly as well. Choose a few pages to visit on a regular basis that will help you build your knowledge about the areas of your business on which you need or want to be knowledgeable. One example is the press release page; this area will help you to stay up to date.

Create a Value Proposition for Your Audience

Regularly reading business publications such as the *Wall Street Journal* allows you to educate yourself on business in general; you learn what other organizations are doing and can build general business acumen, which makes you a more valuable partner. You create what's called a *value proposition* for your audience.

Finally, mentors and your internal clients can help you build your business capabilities. Identify one or two operational leaders to learn from, invite one of them to lunch, and ask open-ended questions about specific initiatives of the business or challenges that the business is facing. You will learn a great deal from how the leader responds to your questions.

Become an Internal Consultant

The road map to consulting capability involves a balance of the following:

- Human resources

- Clients

- Organizational methods

- Center of excellence partners (for example, organizational development professionals)

Building your consulting capability is a more complex exercise than building in the other two areas. These skills require a different mindset from the first two levels.

For many of us, these skills come naturally; we prefer to work in the gray areas rather than using the more clear-cut, black-and-white approach needed for many business capabilities.

When to Step In and When to Stay Out

Consultancy requires you to be patient, allow situations to evolve, and have the judgment to know when to step in and when to stay out. As an internal consultant, you are in the background, facilitating a purposeful outcome without being manipulative and keeping the big picture and organizational objectives as the focus.

Those who can master these types of skills are highly valuable to both the functions and teams they support and the organization as a whole.

Teaching these types of skills can be challenging, but it is not impossible. The first step is to clearly articulate the skills, provide the opportunity to demonstrate them, and then allow for practice in low-risk situations. This coaching can be invaluable.

Kathy Rapp, a senior vice president and managing director at the human resources recruitment and consulting firm hrQ, tells us that business leaders are finding it difficult to identify qualified HR leaders who have the knowledge and skills of a true HR business partner. "CEOs are looking for talent manager senior leaders who understand the business operations and have the ability to lead the design and implementation of talent development strategies that will position the organization to meet its objectives." Rapp adds that these CEOs find that they need to "buy" this talent because human resources functions are not developing enough leaders with these skills and abilities.

Rapp outlines the following success profile for a talent management leader. A progressive organizational development or effectiveness leader needs to have the following knowledge, skills, and abilities to support today's global, complex organizations:

- Have a pragmatic approach to assessment and development.

- Have the knowledge and ability to scale the talent management strategy across large, global organizations.

- Demonstrate a high level of business acumen.

- Have had experience either in or as a true business partner with sales, supply chain, and other core functions.

- Understand how to drive large-scale change throughout the organization.

Admittedly, this is a tall order. However, this is the type of leader who is at the proverbial table that HR is always striving to join.

Where Do You Stand?

Where are you and your HR team on the three-level HRBP model? To find out, conduct an audit focused on each of the three components:

1. HR capabilities

2. Business capabilities

3. Consulting capabilities

Be objective and realistic; stay focused on where you need to go and how to get there—not where you are now.

Make a plan, commit to it, execute it, and measure your progress. Use your internal clients as your gauge. Keep the points in Table 3.2 in mind as you navigate the playing field.

Table 3.2 **Dos and Don'ts for HR Business Partners**	
Always	**Never**
• Act as a responsible agent of the organization	• Focus on process over people
• Balance the needs and expectations of your stakeholders	• Be afraid to take a calculated risk
• Trust your intuition	• Lose your balance between your stakeholders
• Demonstrate your understanding of the business through your decisions and actions	• Miss an opportunity to use your skills and role to address an issue

We heard the need for upgrading HR team members' skills from several human resources executives we spoke to for this book. Johnni Beckel at OhioHealth identified the need to help those on her human resources team understand what the organization needs from them, and then provide them with the skills and experiences to meet those needs. "I challenge my team to go where the pull is and ride the coattails of a leader who is leading the way for change and/or key initiatives." The only way for Human Resources to have the ability to do this is to be connected to leaders in the organization and have a deep understanding of the business. To support her team's development, Beckel is working with an expert to customize a best-practice program focused on developing the skills needed for her human resources team at OhioHealth.

Coaches Come in All Shapes and Sizes

Although the HRBP plays a central role in the assessment and development strategy and programs in most organizations, we cannot forget about the additional roles that are needed in order for the programs to be implemented and the goals realized. Let's talk through the leaders and managers.

HRBPs and Managers

You can design a fantastic best-practice development program, but if the leaders and managers in your organization are not engaged and can't see the value in the program, you will see neither an impact nor a return on the investment. There are several consequences of this scenario, such as loss of credibility, wasted resources, and employees who are not provided with opportunities to develop and grow in ways that will support the needs of the business.

To avoid this scenario, it is important to know how and when to involve and engage your managers and leaders.

If your organization leverages the HRBP, you have a built-in resource to help you both understand and engage leaders and managers. Remember that the HRBP model positions the human resources business partner as a liaison between the business and the human resources function (see Figure 3.2).

Figure 3.2

Business Leaders ⟷ **HRBP** ⟷ **HR Experts**

Define the leaders' and managers' role as part of the assessment and development, educate them, and provide them with the support and resources that they need if they are to be successful.

A best-practice role definition for leaders and human resources partners is to engage in the development of their team members. This approach is often referred to as leader as coach. Personnel Decisions International (PDI, now a part of Korn/Ferry) conducted research on the amount of time a manager needs to dedicate to the development of her team in order to be effective. They found that if a leader dedicates 5 percent of her time to actively coaching and developing, the team and individuals will see a real effect. This research was done in response to the most common excuse given by managers when they are asked to coach team members: "I don't have enough time." When presented with the 5 percent number, it is difficult for leaders to argue that they cannot carve out such a small amount of their time for coaching and developing.

When you position your leaders and managers to play the role of coach, they are responsible for the following:

1. Understanding the developmental needs of each team member

2. Communicating those needs to the team member

3. Providing the resources and opportunities that will allow the team member to grow and develop

4. Sharing constructive and actionable feedback

5. Holding team members accountable for reaching their development objectives

Of course, this model requires your manager to have the necessary skills to play the role of coach successfully. We will outline a best-practice approach for assessing and developing your managers and leaders in Chapter 4.

The following steps enable the HR team to partner effectively with managers to:

1. Identify the success profile for the overall team and each role within the team.

2. Assess the team and its members against the success profile.

3. Use the assessment to bring strengths and gaps to the surface.

4. Identify the appropriate experiences, tools, resources, and development programs needed to address the gaps.

5. Coach and support the manager as he carries out his role.

This approach allows each participant—the HRBP and the leader/manager—to leverage her strengths and partner with others to address gaps: a true partnership!

HRBPs and ODs, TMs, or LDs

Another member of the coaching staff is the organizational development (OD), talent management (TM), or leadership development (LD) expert. In many mid- and large-sized organizations, this role has its own department within the human resources function. In smaller organizations, the HRBP or generalist may be responsible for the OD and/or LD responsibilities and outcomes. Many organizations, regardless of their size, also rely on external resources to supplement or sometimes own the OD or LD needs of the organization.

Any of these structures can work successfully. The key is for the leadership to understand what works best for the unique needs and structure of the organization. The next critical step is to clearly define and communicate the roles.

Let's take a step back and clearly outline the role of an OD, LD, or TM expert.

Richard Beckhard, an early leader in the field, defined organizational development as follows:

"OD is an effort that is planned, organization wide and managed from the top, to increase organizational effectiveness and health through planned interventions in the organization process, using behavioral science knowledge."

Beckhard's definition was published in 1969 and is still relevant and applicable today. It supports our position that assessment and development initiatives must support the business and confirms that OD professionals bring expertise in a unique and specific area of behavioral science to the human resources function. This expertise, combined with a strong understanding and knowledge of the business from the HRBP and/or operational business leaders, creates the partnership needed for successful development strategies and programs.

CASE STUDY

OhioHealth

Here is an example of how one organization partners with its leaders and managers to drive purposeful development.

Three times each year, OhioHealth brings together approximately 1,000 of its top leaders for a half-day leadership forum led by the organization's CEO. The primary purpose of these events is to reinforce OhioHealth's vision by presenting key initiatives that the organization is embarking on to support the vision. The CEO and selected individuals leading various initiatives convey the importance of each leader's taking ownership of driving the initiatives and enabling the vision to become a reality. In addition to outlining the roles and responsibilities of leadership, OhioHealth gives the leaders the resources and support they need for success. Johnni Beckel shared that the theme of an upcoming leadership forum is "Access to Care." Using a variety of learning methods, such as presentations, small group discussion, and skits, the session will outline the expectations for leaders from of all parts of the health-care system to identify how they affect access to care. Are they enablers, or do they get in the way? The connection made between each leader's actions and the achievement of initiatives, such as Access to Care, drives high levels of employee engagement at OhioHealth and has led to an impressive jump from sixty-ninth to thirty-fifth on *Fortune*'s list of 100 Best Companies to Work For.

Beckel and her team have a clear role both in working closely with the leadership to identify and communicate the key initiatives and in supporting the work and development needs that happen beyond the leadership forums.

HR's role is to design and implement effective development strategies and programs to ensure that leaders have both the knowledge and encouragement to carry out initiatives.

HRBPs and Senior Leaders

The final coaching role we will explore is that of the senior leader. What is a senior leader? Generally, the senior or executive leadership is defined as the CEO or president and her or his direct reports. Some organizations may also include the next layer of senior executives or executive vice presidents.

What do you need your senior leaders to do with regard to your assessment and development efforts? Many HR professionals either over, or underestimate what senior leaders should do to support development strategies and programs. When the role is overestimated—meaning that HR believes that the senior leaders should play a broad role—HR is almost always disappointed. When the role is underestimated, programs may either not take hold or not realize their potential.

The retail case study in Chapter 2 provides an example of how to engage and leverage the role of senior leaders effectively. One reason for this balance is that the HRBPs are truly business partners. This relationship opens the door to engaging senior leaders in the appropriate way.

Another best-practice example of an effective partnership between HR and senior leadership is at a firm called WD Partners, an architecture and design firm that creates solutions for retail organizations. Melissa Buller, the HR director, has a strong and proven relationship and partnership with the organization's president, Chris Doerschlag. Doerschlag trusts Buller's expertise as a partner and her ability to develop and deliver development initiatives that support his strategies and the overall needs of the organization. For a growing company with a diverse population of employees, designing a development strategy that meets a broad range of needs is a challenge. Buller and Doerschlag agreed to focus on one or two core development objectives that support the long-term strategy.

WD's business was significantly affected by the 2008–2011 recession that much of our country experienced. Because of smart business decisions, strong partnerships, and good leadership, WD emerged from this challenge as a leader in its field. It is now growing and has been hiring new employees to support its growth.

This recent growth has brought in new talent that did not experience the challenges that the recession brought, and while it was dealing with the recession, the organization was razor focused on building client relationships and stopped investing time and resources in integrating new associates into the company's strong culture.

Doerschlag and Buller realized that it was critical to ensure that the organization's practices and culture support its long-term objectives. To make sure that he had a clear understanding of how employees were thinking and feeling about the organization and how they were getting work done, Doerschlag decided to talk with them; these discussions were termed "Gab and Grabs."

Several positive outcomes emerged from this hands-on needs assessment. An obvious benefit was the interaction between Doerschlag and the employees. This is a rare opportunity that most leaders never leverage in a meaningful way. The key development need that surfaced during the Gab and Grabs was WD business acumen. Like many organizations that were affected by market conditions, WD had discontinued some of the development practices that had allowed associates to understand the unique way the company conducts business with its clients. This gap became apparent in the discussions that Doerschlag was having. In addition, he understood the need to address and support further development of technical and functional skills. This gap created work process and project management challenges.

The assessment gave Buller and her team WD's organizational development objectives for the coming year. They are currently designing programs that will position the associates at WD to bridge these gaps and position the organization to continue to differentiate itself in the marketplace.

Buller's strategy includes a two-track development program that is scalable and that supports meaningful engagement and retention:

- *Track 1* is technical training and continuing education opportunities specific to WD's designers, architects, engineers, program managers, and support associates.

- *Track 2* is an experiential program that builds associates' knowledge of how WD does business, creates opportunities to enhance soft skills, and provides learning opportunities outside of the "9-5."

As the senior leader, Doerschlag increased the likelihood of success through his sponsorship of the development initiatives that lend credibility and accountability.

Buller and Doerschlag's example illustrates both a strong and aligned partnership between HR and senior leadership and the key role of a senior leader: sponsorship. When the senior leader actively sponsors the development strategy and initiatives, the rest of the organization will engage and participate. Absence of senior leader sponsorship can cause the broader leadership to question the relevance of development programs and lead to inconsistent participation. This, of course, leads to suboptimization of programs and unrealized objectives. HR needs to strike the right balance with senior leadership, build credibility, and facilitate active sponsorship.

Defining and managing the role of each participant in your organization's assessment and development strategy is critical for success. As with many things in organizations that seem straightforward, accomplishing this can be a real challenge.

Know When to Call In Partners

After taking a hit during the recession as individuals and companies cut nonessential spending, demand for business coaching has picked up significantly in the past 24 months. Leaders and human resources professionals are again investing in external coaches, as well as increasing the capabilities and capacity of their internal coaching resources. The value and impact of coaching has often been difficult to measure, calling into question the return on the investment. With the return of coaching, many organizations have learned how to ask the right questions to identify both coaching resources that meet the needs of their leaders and how they will measure the impact of the coaching.

A recent *Harvard Business Review* article provided the following data related to using professional coaches.[3]

THE TOP THREE REASONS COACHES ARE ENGAGED

- To develop high potentials or facilitate transition: 48 percent

- To act as a sounding board: 26 percent

- To address derailing behavior: 12 percent

How Much Does Coaching Cost?

- $300–$500 (and higher) per hour for a high-quality executive coach

Who Is Involved in the Coaching Process?

- The manager

- Human Resources

- The coachee

- Others

Who Initiates the Coaching?

- The manager: 23 percent

- Human Resources: 29.5 percent

- The coachee: 28.8 percent

- Others: 18.7 percent

Who Is Kept Apprised of Progress?

- The coachee: 87.9 percent

- Managers: 67.9 percent

- Human Resources: 55.7 percent

- Others: 21.1 percent

How Long Is the Coaching Engagement?

- Between 7 and 12 months

Industry Statistics

ActionCOACH Consulting compiled the following industry statistics and general overview of the value and ROI that executive coaching offer. The survey data are from executives who work in large (mostly Fortune 1,000) companies who had participated in either "change-oriented" coaching, aimed at improving certain behaviors or skills, or "growth-oriented" coaching, designed to sharpen overall job performance. The programs lasted from six months to a year. About 60 percent of the executives were aged 40 to 49, a prime age bracket for career retooling. One-half of the respondents held positions of vice president or higher, and a third earned $200,000 or more per year.

- In one study conducted by MetrixGlobal LLC, companies including Booz Allen Hamilton received an average return of $7.90 for every $1 invested in executive coaching.

- A recent study by MetrixGlobal of executive coaching in a Fortune 500 firm reported a 529 percent return on investment and significant intangible benefits to the business.

- A survey of 100 executives by Manchester Inc. found that coaching provided an average return on investment of almost six times the cost of the coaching.

- An internal report of the Personnel Management Association showed that when training is combined with coaching, individuals increase their productivity by an average of 86 percent, compared to 22 percent with training alone.

- A Hay Group study of Fortune 500 companies found that 21 to 40 percent utilize executive coaching. Coaching was used as part of standard leadership development for elite executives and talented up-and-comers.

- A 2001 study on the impact of executive coaching by Manchester Inc. showed an average ROI of 5.7 times the initial investment or a return of more than $100,000, according to executives who estimated the monetary value of the results achieved through coaching. Among the benefits to the companies that provided coaching were:

- Productivity (reported by 53 percent of executives)

- Quality (48 percent)

- Organizational strength (48 percent)

- Customer service (39 percent)

- Reducing customer complaints (34 percent)

- Retaining executives who received coaching (32 percent)

- Cost reductions (23 percent)

- Bottom-line profitability (22 percent)

- Among the benefits to executives who received coaching were improved:

  - Working relationships with direct reports (reported by 77 percent of executives)

  - Working relationships with immediate supervisors (71 percent)

  - Teamwork (67 percent)

- Working relationships with peers (63 percent)

- Job satisfaction (61 percent)

- Conflict reduction (52 percent)

- Organizational commitment (44 percent)

- Working relationships with clients (37 percent)

Putting the Stats into Action

The statistics give us a view of coaching best practices that lead to high-impact results. It is now time to outline a methodology that positions the coachee for success.

It is important to begin by determining what your organization's philosophy and guidelines for leadership coaching are. Use the following set of questions to help you with the discussion:

1. Why do we believe that leadership coaching will benefit our leaders?

2. How do we define leadership coaching?

3. What types of development situations should qualify for coaching?

4. Will we use internal or external coaches, or both?

5. How will we qualify our coaches?

6. What type of information and feedback will we expect from our coaches?

7. What role will Human Resources play?

8. What role will the coachee's manager play?

9. What fee structure do we feel fits for our organizations?

10. Who can initiate a coaching project?

11. Do we want a uniform approach to coaching, or can each coach and coachee create a unique approach?

12. Should our leadership competencies be integrated into leadership coaching?

13. How will we manage the information and/or any documentation that results from coaching projects?

14. What does a successful coaching project look like?

The answers to these questions and others that are specific to your organization will give you the information you need to form your philosophy and guidelines for initiating and managing leadership coaching in a way that benefits your leaders and is aligned with your culture.

Now that you have the foundation, you can move on to create a methodology. Anne and Brenda use a best-practice coaching process based on the following.

Successful Coaching Requires A(n):

- Partnership between the coachee, her manager, Human Resources, and the coach

- Clear understanding of the coaching objectives

- Agreed-upon beginning and end

- Clearly articulated desired state

- Method for measuring progress

We applied these principles in our innovative and practical coaching process (see Table 3.3).

Table 3.3 **The Coaching Process**	
Coaching Process Phase	**Action**
Discovery	Define the current state and scope
Define success	Clearly articulate the coaching outcomes
	(continues)

Table 3.3 **The Coaching Process** (continued)	
Coaching Process Phase	**Action**
Develop the road map	Align all stakeholders, including coachee, manager, Human Resources, and coach
Develop the individual coaching plan	Create an individual coaching plan to meet the objectives
Implement the coaching road map	Coach the leader and support stakeholders
Evaluate and update	Review the progress of the coaching against objectives
Summary and recommendations	Provide a record of the coaching process and recommendations for next steps

As we noted earlier, measurement is a key component of the coaching process and keeps all stakeholders accountable for their roles within the coaching partnership. Table 3.3 is an example of a tool to track the progress of the coaching work.

TIPS AND TAKEAWAYS FROM THIS CHAPTER

- Clearly outline coaching roles and responsibilities.

- Understand and implement the true definition of a human resources business partner.

- Assess your current standings.

- Leverage your special team players.

- Position your senior leaders for success.

CHAPTER 4

The Roster

No one can whistle a symphony. It takes an orchestra to play it.

—H. E. Luccock

Y ou have undoubtedly heard and talked about the fact that the U.S. workforce has never been as diverse as it is today. We have as many as five generations and multiple cultures, all working side by side.

Most organizations are aware of the dynamics that result from having a diverse organization; however, human resources and senior leaders need to identify ways to leverage these differences instead of allowing them to get in the way.

A full discussion of workforce diversity would take an entire book of its own. Let's focus on a key set of populations in today's workplace and outline assessment and development strategies for each. The populations we'll focus on are new employees, new leaders, and each of the five generations that work in today's organizations.

Rookies

Let's start at the beginning with new employees. Before the 2008 recession, most organizations were adding onboarding programs to their talent management strategies. Research conducted by pioneers in this work—such as Diane Downey, whose research was the basis for the book *Assimilating New Leaders: The Key to Executive Retention*,[1] and Michael Watkins's *The First 90 Days: Critical Success Strategies for New Leaders at All Levels*[2]—brought to the surface what many leaders already knew: there is a significant amount of cost and missed opportunity when onboarding is left to chance. The Aberdeen Group was the first research organization to demonstrate the link among purposeful onboarding, employee engagement, and productivity in its report *Onboarding: The First Line of Engagement*.[3] Before the development of effective onboarding programs, organizations, and specifically hiring managers, were frustrated when a new hire failed to perform either at the level or in the time frame that was needed. However, hiring managers and Human Resources often saw this issue as part of the cost of doing business. This dynamic also caused finger-pointing between HR and the leaders for either not recruiting the right talent effectively or not training and integrating talent effectively. Once onboarding came into our vernacular and then our practice, organizations began to take notice of the cost of poor onboarding processes and experience.

Figure 4.1 was developed from the research conducted by Watkins. It illustrates the real effect of a structured onboarding program.

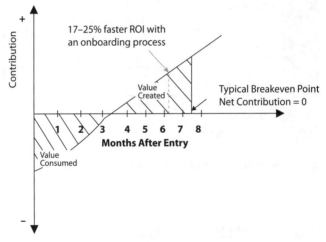

Figure 4.1 **Effects of Structured Onboarding Programs**

Putting the Data to Work

In response to the business case that this research provided, HR professionals began to develop onboarding programs in partnership with a growing pool of experts in the marketplace.

The six-step model in Figure 4.2 outlines a road map for building an onboarding program that fits the specific needs of your organization.

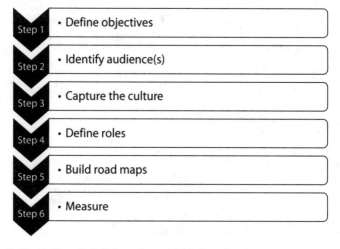

Step 1 • Define objectives

Step 2 • Identify audience(s)

Step 3 • Capture the culture

Step 4 • Define roles

Step 5 • Build road maps

Step 6 • Measure

Figure 4.2 **Steps in Building a Successful Onboarding Program**

Create a Level Playing Field

Once you have an effective employee onboarding program, it is important that you address the unique challenges and needs of each population so that you keep people engaged throughout the onboarding period that connects and into the development phase of talent management. The only way to create a level playing field that supports each population's success is to meet the people in that population where they are.

Just as with onboarding, it is critical that you have an overall strategy that allows for customization based on the audience *and* that stays rooted in your organization's strategy.

Leaders and Managers

Let's examine the leadership population next. Generally speaking, leaders make up 10 percent of an organization. The roles and responsibilities of this population, in addition to the effect of its performance and decisions on the organization, tell us that it makes sense to identify strategies that address the unique challenges of this population.

Again, we will start at the beginning, with recruitment and onboarding. These processes combined with the organization's experience with leaders in their first six months give you a baseline body of knowledge on each new leader. This baseline can then be leveraged to identify a development plan that allows each leader to reach his or her potential.

Remember that the talent management cycle in Chapter 1 begins with selection, followed by onboarding. Performance management and leadership development pick up after onboarding. An effective talent management strategy positions each of these phases to build upon the previous one.

CASE STUDY

The Ohio State University

Cindy Silver, Director of Organization & Leadership Effectiveness at The Ohio State University (OSU), is responsible for providing development support to the university's top leaders. One of Silver and her team's core offerings is a 12-month executive onboarding program. OSU's onboarding program focuses on the executive's successful integration into the university and his or her role. Key components of the program include:

- Establishing and achieving onboarding objectives

- Building the right relationships

- Understanding how to navigate the culture successfully

   A university is a complex academic environment that can easily trip up even the most seasoned leader. This is especially true when the new leader comes from the private sector or some other nonacademic organization. Throughout each leader's first year, Silver builds a strong relationship with that leader and develops an in-depth understanding of her or his strengths and challenges, and those of her or his team. This positions Silver and her team to develop strategies to meet each leader's unique needs.

Silver and her team of organizational development professionals have leveraged the relationships built through the onboarding engagement into a broader partnership with leaders across the university. This partnership has led to an innovative approach to supporting leaders through difficult situations. The OD consultant team offers what it calls Insight Sessions. These sessions give leaders the opportunity to bring a significant challenge that they are struggling with to a private working session. The Insight Sessions are structured, yet they can accommodate each unique leader and his or her challenge. Silver articulated the objective of each session: "The objective of each session is to give leaders insight into the dilemma before prescribing a solution." She said that when leaders refer to their issues, they often tell her, "I never looked at it that way."

Silver shared, "As a team, our vision is that no leader is ever stuck. This helps us to not judge their issue or challenge, and the Insight Sessions give us a highly effective vehicle to act on this vision."

(continues)

> Although the academic setting is unique, the practices and outcomes are certainly applicable to leadership populations in any type of organization. Silver and her team understood the need to meet each leader where he or she is and customized the approach by drawing on a set of tools that are aligned with the culture and the organizational objectives.

To further support the leadership population, organizations have increased the investment they are making in leadership development. Kathy Rapp, senior vice president and managing director of a human resources consulting firm headquartered in Denver, told us that she has observed a resurgence of internal assessment centers. These centers are often part of an internal "university" structure, which Rapp said is also making a comeback. Assessment centers are typically part of the talent management function and include technical, soft-skill, leadership, sales, and knowledge worker development.

The Talent Pool

There are five generations in today's organizations; let's begin with some definitions to provide a common understanding and language.

Table 4.1 outlines the five generations and provides insight into their views that affect how they interact in the workplace.

Table 4.1 **Characteristics of Generations**		
Generation	**Birth Year**	**Characteristics**
Traditionalists	Before 1945	• Influenced by the Great Depression • Loyal • Respect authority
Baby boomers	After World War II through 1960	• Embrace corporate structure • Comfortable with formality • Prefer to be in charge
Generation X	1961–1981	• Value having options • Mistrust corporate structure • Bring strong relationship skills
Millennial (Generation Y)	1982–1997	• Raised with technology • Comfortable with a global, multicultural world • Value personal time and pursuits
Generation 2020	After 1997	• Technologically dependent • Closely tied to parents • Tolerant of alternative lifestyles

How is each generation represented in the workplace? The employment projections report shown in Figure 4.3 gives us a picture of the generational makeup of our current workforce and projects how it will look in the year 2020.

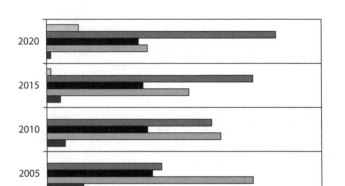

Figure 4.3 **Five Generations in the Workplace**

Source: Bureau of Labor Statistics Employment Projections.

Although these data may not be surprising, they do give leaders and human resources professionals a view of the different types of employees they are and will be leading and developing over the next several years.

Each generation has different expectations regarding effective development initiatives that will help them achieve their goals. Human resources leaders have struggled to come up with an approach that meets the expectations of all these groups. When we talked with a human resources business partner at an off-priced retailer, he shared this challenge: "How do we customize development plans for the millennial population without losing our core culture, norms, and overall balance?"

To further illustrate both the differences and the similarities of the different generations, the technology firm SAP conducted a survey that asked members of the three most prevalent generations five different questions. Figure 4.4 is a summary of the responses.

How do these answers reflect those in your organization? If you are not sure, bring groups of employees together and find out.

The Batter at the Plate

What role does the individual employee, regardless of generation, play in his or her own development? Many organizations expect employees to drive their own development while the organization provides the opportunity and resources. What does this look like?

As described earlier, many younger employees believe that they understand what type(s) of development they need in order to build the type of résumé needed for their next role(s). In addition, they expect their manager and their organization to provide the opportunities that they need if they are to obtain those skills and experiences. The first step is determining whether the employee's list of development needs is the same as his or her manager's and the organization's lists. The following are talking

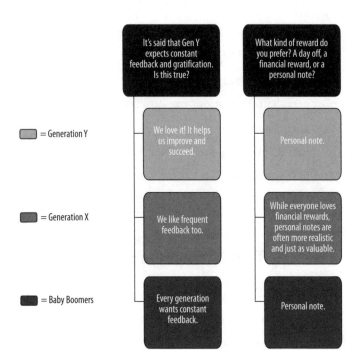

Figure 4.4 **Five Questions for Generation Y, Generation X, and Baby Boomers About the Work World**

points that a manager can use to understand what the employee believes are important and then to realign the employee if needed.

- "I am interested in understanding the skills and development experiences you feel are important for you to focus on in the next 12 months."

- "Let's begin with the skills and behaviors that are needed for your current role."

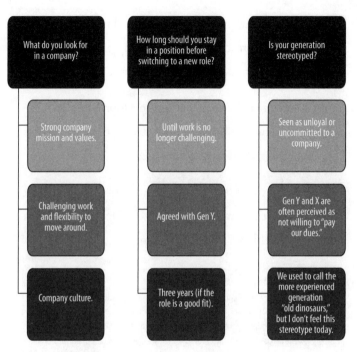

Figure 4.4 *(continued)*

- Use active listening as the employee shares this list.

- Summarize what you heard the employee say.

- "I agree that you would benefit from further development of. . . ."

- "In addition, shadowing one of our operations leaders in the warehouse will give you a clearer understanding of how our department and the warehouse are connected and the work that needs to be done to improve the handoffs between us."

- "Based on our previous discussions, I understand that you are interested in moving into an analyst role in the next 12 to 18 months. Is that still your goal?"

- "Okay, great. We can use our development plan template to outline development strategies for both your short-term and long-term objectives."

Step 2 is providing a structure for the development strategies, as well as tracking progress. The development plan template in Table 4.2 provides for both.

Table 4.2 **Development Plan Template**
This process is designed to support the development of competencies and skills to facilitate your success. Please complete a plan for each of the competencies and skills (up to two) that you have identified as development opportunities.
Review the completed plan with your manager, seek resources to support the desired development, and target the timeline listed to complete your plan.
Name: Job Title:
Development Goal 1:
What are the potential barriers to meeting this objective? What strategies will you use to address these barriers?
Barriers: Strategies:

What strengths will you leverage to address your objective?
What support resources will you use for this objective?
On-the-Job Assignments   Training   Network   Professional Coach
How will you know when you have reached your objective?

TIPS AND TAKEAWAYS FROM THIS CHAPTER

- Give your rookies a solid foundation with an effective onboarding program.

- Identify the unique needs of your leadership population.

- Leverage the diversity of the multiple generations in your organization.

- Anticipate the assessment and development needs you will have in the future.

- Engage your employees in development discussions and provide them with a structure with which to manage their own development.

CHAPTER 5

The Game Changer: Millennials

Conformity is the last refuge of the
unimaginative.

—OSCAR WILDE

The arrival of this generation on the workplace scene started a revolution! Most organizations responded with a bit of shock and awe that quickly turned to anger and frustration. Leaders called upon their human resources partners to "get these young employees into line." However, organizations soon realized that this generation was neither going away nor planning to conform to traditional norms.

Given the significant effect that this generation has had on the overall workforce, it warrants their own chapter of strategies and case studies to help you leverage the unique skill sets and strengths that this group brings.

Outspoken Millennials

At a 2013 town hall meeting, the CEO of a large, multidivision organization found herself in a situation she had never been in before. During the question-and-answer portion of the meeting, several young employees asked the CEO very direct questions. These employees wanted to know specifics about the CEO's expansion plans, and what opportunities would be available to them and when. Once the CEO was off the stage, she asked her head of HR, "Who do they think they are?"

Clearly taken aback by the directness of the employees' questions and the amount of information that they obviously felt they were entitled to, the CEO struggled with this new reality that she and her leadership team were facing. As she and her HR executive returned to her office after the town hall meeting, she realized that the senior executive team needed to figure out the right way to engage this group, one that would allow them to feel empowered yet not overstep their roles. These employees were the future, and the CEO realized that if her organization didn't leverage what they had to offer, another organization would.

The millennial generation was influenced by several events and phenomena that shaped the way they approach work and the expectations they have of their employers. A key event was 9/11. Most millennials were in grade school when the United States was attacked; therefore, they do not remember our country before this horrific event. This, of course, shaped who they are and what they want for themselves and their families. In addition, these young men and women grew up in a time of prosperity; both of their parents worked and had the financial resources to provide their children, the millennials, with the latest and greatest toys and experiences. They were also taught to respect authority, but also not to fear it and to ask teachers, physicians, and coaches for what they needed. This is the generation in which everyone received a ribbon regardless of how well he or she performed. These expectations come into the workplace with the millennials.

CASE STUDY

A Unique Retail Approach

As merchant-led organizations, most retailers invest significant resources in merchant training and development. As the off-priced retail human resources business partner has found, participants in his company's early merchant development programs are very demanding. "Millennials in our merchant organization are always looking to move through the development programs quickly and want more and more responsibilities. They tell me, 'I already have these skills, and we need to keep moving.'"

Four Strategies to Engage Millennials

Many talent management and organizational development professionals we talked with for this book had had similar experiences. To address this challenge, these professionals have identified four key strategies to engage millennials in the development process.

1. *Accept.* This is an important population, and it is here to stay. Accept the fact that the organization needs these people for short- and long-term success.

2. *Interact.* Create the opportunity to talk with leaders and managers about ways to accept and embrace this generation that are not threatening.

    a. Organize breakfast or lunch discussions with a combination of millennials and other generations. Provide some structure to these discussions to facilitate positive experiences.

    b. Develop opportunities for millennials to shadow more experienced leaders. Coach each to support a positive outcome.

3. *Engage.* Include millennials in the design of your on-boarding and development curriculum. Use a structured approach to gather their input. Ask questions such as:

    a. How do you best learn?

    b. How do you want to receive feedback on your progress?

    c. What role do you expect your manager to play in your development?

    d. What skills and experiences are most important for you to add to your toolbox in the next one to three years?

By engaging in this dialogue with your young talent, you will also have the opportunity to educate them on the culture of the organization, what's realistic, and the expectations you have of them.

4. *Deliver.* Organizations that do not provide development opportunities for their millennials will lose them. Another consequence is that they may create their own developmental opportunities, which may not be aligned with the organization's culture or values.

Organizational development leaders are also addressing the development needs of these key populations as they present themselves in team dynamics.

CASE STUDY

Mean Girls

An OD director at a leading specialty retailer shared an example of a challenge she was working through that involved several members of a team. Let's refer to the group as Team M.

Team M consisted of six young women, all of whom were in either their first or their second job out of college.

All of these women were very talented and strong performers. In the past three months, however, the members of Team M had been exhibiting disruptive and unprofessional behavior directed at one another. The leader of Team M sought out the director of OD to talk through possible ways to address the dynamics of this team, which of course was getting in the way of productivity.

The OD director conducted interviews with each team member and was quite astonished by some of what she heard from the members of Team M! Many of these women justified their behavior because they saw themselves as being more intelligent and better performers than their peers. They did not feel any responsibility for changing the overall dynamics of the team.

The team leader was committed to working with his team; he simply had no idea of where to begin.

The OD director designed a blended approach, one that focused on understanding and applying healthy behaviors to create healthy and productive work relationships, and developing ways to respond to and manage unhealthy behavior and relationships at work. Additionally, the OD director and Team M's leader identified a need to clarify workflow roles and the handoffs between the

(continues)

team members. To address this need, they designed working sessions to map out the workflow and discuss roles and handoffs. These working sessions also provided the team members and the leader and OD director with opportunities to reinforce healthy team behaviors and coaching opportunities when unhealthy behaviors popped up.

Upon reflection, both the team leader and the OD director believed that one source of the team's dysfunctional behavior stemmed from its members' habit of sharing their direct opinions and thoughts through social media and other social interactions, in addition to the coaching and direction that they had received throughout their lives to focus on what they need and want and their need to actively compete for those things. Although a bit extreme, this is an excellent example of how this OD leader could take advantage of a dynamic that was taking place in her organization, engage both the leadership and millennials, and turn it into a development opportunity that balanced the employees' expectations with the culture and values of the organization.

Invite Mom and Dad!

When she was an HR executive at a national fast food restaurant chain, Johnni Beckel was working with restaurant managers who were experiencing 200 percent turnover in their restaurants. Most restaurant employees were high school students who would quickly leave their job for an additional $0.25 per hour at another fast food company down the street. To address this challenge, the idea of holding a Parent's Night at the restaurants surfaced. Managers closed the restaurant for the event and talked with parents about how important their children were to the restaurant, its ability to offer flexible schedules to accommodate school requirements, and its general interest in providing the kids with a good work experience and life skills. These events had an enormously positive effect on the turnover rate at these restaurants. Turnover decreased by 35 percent! Parents felt that they had a connection with the restaurant managers, which led to discussions if a scheduling or other issue came up. The restaurant brand understood the influence that the parents of millennials have and invited them into the workplace instead of focusing only on the hourly rate.

TIPS AND TAKEAWAYS FROM THIS CHAPTER

- The one-size-fits-all approach will not work!

- Follow these four steps to capture and motivate your millennials:

  1. Accept

  2. Interact

  3. Engage

  4. Deliver

CHAPTER 6

Keep It Current!

Success seems to be connected with action. Successful people keep moving. They make mistakes, but they don't quit.

—Conrad Hilton, Hilton Hotels

The worst thing that HR partners and leaders can do is to allow themselves to become irrelevant to the people they are responsible for developing.

Stay in the Know

HR leaders are expected to be aware of and understand how to leverage current assessment and development trends and tools within the organizations that they support. You have heard us express the importance of having strong business acumen skills and leveraging those skills to do your work as an HR and organizational development professional. Keeping yourself up-to-date on the latest trends and determining whether those new tools may add value to your organization is a part of that expectation. In addition, it keeps you motivated and interested in our field.

Take a Balanced Approach

We all know colleagues who are attracted to a shiny new tool—that newest, latest, and greatest thing. Those people are always on the lookout for a trendy approach, methodology, or product that they can introduce and try out so that they can be seen as trailblazers. However, this can be confusing and risky to both employees and the reputation of the individual who is serving up the "flavor of the month."

It is important to balance your interest in the latest trend with what the organization needs and its culture.

Leveraging Methodologies

Zoe Klopf Switzer, director of organizational development at a specialty retailer, shared how she has been successful at integrating concepts and tools into different cultures.

Prior to her current role Klopf Switzer worked as a consultant and had the opportunity to gain expertise in several development methodologies. She developed expertise and saw how these methodologies drove results in many different types of organizations. Klopf Switzer also learned that she could leverage different methods without putting a label on the work that might not fit with the organization she was supporting. In addition, her experience allowed her to create a customized approach for each organization and each situation within that organization.

Klopf Switzer is an example of an organizational development professional who understands how to stay current in her field and leverage her knowledge to meet the needs of the population(s) for whom she is responsible.

Keeping Leaders Current

Just as there is an expectation that human resources and organizational development professionals will stay current, leaders are also expected to continue to evolve with the market and with workforce needs and dynamics. Not doing so threatens not only the longevity of the individual leader but also the sustained success of the organization. So how do leaders avoid becoming complacent?

1. *Be open.* We must be open to the idea that there are better ways to do things. If we believe that we already have the best answers, we will miss the next new idea, which can be a game changer.

2. *Stay curious.* Healthy curiosity leads to strategic thinking.

3. *Be vulnerable.* Unless we allow ourselves to admit that we do not have all the best ideas and solutions and to invite others in to share their ideas and options, we will not benefit from what others have to offer.

4. *Take chances.* "Take chances, make mistakes. That's how you grow. Pain nourishes your courage. You have to fail in order to practice being brave."—Mary Tyler Moore

5. *Be patient.* We often underestimate how long it can take for real change and progress to take place. Give new ideas a chance to take hold.

Both human resources professionals and leaders need to step outside of their own organizations to stay current on trends and solutions that may have a positive effect and serve as a solution for the real business issues they are facing.

Choosing two to three of the following to add to your own development strategy will keep you in the starting lineup:

- ***Read.*** Choose specialized publications, blogs, or sites that focus on development and general business sources that report strategies, methodologies, and tools and how they are being applied. Examples include:

  - *Talent Management* magazine

  - *Workforce* magazine

  - Conference Board talent management report

  - http://blog.talentmgt.com

  - logs.ddiworld.com

  - *Wall Street Journal*

  - *Fast Company*

  - *Harvard Business Review*

  - *New York Times* business section

  - *Financial Times*

  - *Mindful Magazine*

  - *Fortune* and *Forbes* magazines

  These are, of course, only a few of the many, many sources for development information and how it is applied. Choose your favorites and add them to your regular reading list.

- *Get out there!* Go to conferences, professional presentations, and other organizations that are getting the results that you want. It is easy to get caught up in how your organization is doing things, especially if you are on one end of the success spectrum or the other—highly successful or in a crisis. Navel-gazing is a not a good strategy. Just as we outlined with reading resources, identify opportunities in the marketplace that keep you current. Possibilities include:

  - Professional organization conferences

  - Leadership forums

  - Business school executive programs

  The publications and blogs that you choose to add to your list are a great resource for identifying these opportunities.

- *Work the room.* How robust is your professional network? Do you have regular conversations with peers, mentors, mentees, and colleagues inside and outside of your current organization? If you answer anything but a clear *yes*, you need to dedicate time to building a mutually beneficial network. Too many of us pay attention to our network only when we need a new job; that approach is shortsighted and benefits only you. Consider the following to build an active and rewarding professional network.

- *Be awesome.* We all want to be around other people who are positive and energetic and who do things for us. Be one of those whom others want to be around.

- *Be helpful.* Take opportunities to do things for others that help them reach their objectives. Most of us are happy to help others and gain satisfaction just from doing so.

- *Be intentional.* Who should be in your network? How will you build a relationship with these individuals? In 2012, *Forbes* published a list of the top 10 people who should be in your network that still holds true today:

  1. The mentor

  2. The coach

  3. The industry insider

  4. The trendsetter

  5. The connector

6. The idealist

7. The realist

8. The visionary

9. The partner

10. The wannabe

- *Be patient.* Developing an effective professional network takes time, and the network evolves over time. By following these steps and keeping at it, you will have a network that is mutually beneficial and pays long-term dividends.

- *Get feedback.* The only way to get a truly accurate view of how you are doing is to ask for feedback. Make it easy for colleagues and members of your network to give you objective and actionable feedback. Use these questions to pave the way for useful feedback:

  - I have been working on (insert skill or behavior). How do you think I am doing with this skill?

  - As a participant in our new leadership initiative, I would appreciate your input regarding the first session. What two components do you feel were the most effective and which were the least effective?

- How effective was I when I presented my business case for the second phase of our program?

- What three things should I do to improve my facilitation skills?

All of these questions have three things in common: they are open-ended, situation-specific, and targeted at a specific skill or deliverable.

- *Hit the refresh button.* Schedule an annual checkup for yourself that examines how effective your assessment and development work is relative to the organization's needs. To help you remember, add this checkup to your annual performance review process. Here is a diagnostic to help you stay focused.

  - Which publications are you reading on a regular basis?

  - Have you gained ideas and resources from these publications, and are they still the right ones for you?

  - What conferences and other external events have you attended this year?

  - Did you see a return on your investment of time and money in these external events?

- What is the status of your professional network? Have you added to your network? Have members of your network tapped you as a resource? Whom do you need to add to your network, and how will you achieve this?

- Did you ask for feedback? What did you do with that feedback?

- What is your strategy for keeping up to date in the coming year?

TIPS AND TAKEAWAYS FROM THIS CHAPTER

- Be purposeful about keeping yourself current and relevant.

- Identify outside resources and a personal network that will support your strategy.

- Take risks and try new things.

- Build in a feedback loop to leverage your strengths and address gaps.

CHAPTER 7

The Playbook

Plans are nothing; planning is everything.

—Dwight D. Eisenhower

It's time to pull all the strategies, tips, and tools together into a concise playbook. All coaches, employees, and supporting team members need a well-thought-out plan if they want to cross the finish line successfully.

A theme for an effective playbook emerged through our discussions with human resources and line leaders.

> The bottom line is that you cannot have a one-size-fits-all, off-the-shelf approach. At the same time, organizations' resources are finite and often limited. So it is our job to balance and accommodate all these factors and expectations.

Six Components of the Playbook

The methodology and approach that surfaced through our interview discussions has six components.

Blended Strategy

Kathy Rapp of hrQ works with clients in the oil and gas industry who are pulling their rig supervisors into headquarters for two-day training programs that include several pieces. Rapp described those pieces as involving experiential learning customized to the role and the individual, and prework that reinforces the learning throughout the year.

Experiential Learning

This type of development is playing a prominent role in talent management curricula. Examples of this type of learning vary widely. Melissa Buller at WD Partners, a global design, engineering, and architecture firm that serves the retail and food services industries, shared the experiential initiative that she and her team are designing. The program allows employees to view the WD process from the clients' point of view and experience. Employees learn about both the needs and the perspective of the client, as well as how WD meets those needs.

Customized Approach

To balance the needs of a diverse employee population, organizational development and talent management professionals are providing individuals and teams with customized assessment and development within the organizational development philosophy and framework. Although the drilling supervisors at one of hrQ's oil and gas clients will participate in the supervisory curriculum, a key component of that overall program is a development plan that is specific to each individual supervisor. The plan will focus on how the supervisor will leverage his or her strengths and address gaps that surface during the assessment of his or her talent against a success profile for the role.

Reinforcement and Accountability

We have all heard about the importance of ensuring that development is not just an event, but instead equips employees with knowledge and tools that will have a positive effect on their ability to perform at a higher level, driving overall company success. Talent management and organizational development professionals know that there is a direct correlation between training and development and organizational success. At the same time, professionals have struggled to apply and articulate this correlation. There are countless organizations and resources that can assist you in building the business case for the investment in development. Examples of these resources include the Center for Creative Leadership, the Aberdeen Group, and *Harvard Business Review*, to name just a few. However, leading professionals are taking matters into their own hands and developing curricula that build in accountability and reinforcement. These best-practice curricula include the following core pieces:

- Define objectives.

- Determine participants.

- Develop a communication strategy and plan.

- Bring success profiles for the roles of the participants to the surface.

- Assess participants against the success profile.

- Analyze the strengths and gaps of both the group and individuals.

- Design individual plans and group learning activities that integrate the assessment data.

Engage the Manager

A key to the success of the model outlined here, and of talent development in general, is the active involvement of the manager. By engaging the manager, you also increase the engagement of the employee and the likelihood that the newly learned skills and behaviors will be reinforced on the job. This partnership allows the progress and effectiveness of the development to be measured. Human Resources provides the tools to capture and manage the data and integrate them into the overall management of HR analytics. This work influences future decisions about workforce and development planning.

Customize for the Culture

While this is a more complex methodology, so is today's organizational landscape. It is critical that assessment and development initiatives map out the needs of the organization and the employees that make up that organization. Not doing so puts the organization at risk.

TIPS AND TAKEAWAYS FROM THIS CHAPTER

- One size does not fit all.

- Make learning an experience.

- Build in reinforcement and accountability.

- Engage the coach.

- Don't forget about the unique culture.

CHAPTER 8

Mentoring: A Development Advantage

The best way a mentor can prepare another leader is to expose him or her to other great people.

—JOHN C. MAXWELL

Do you have a professional mentor? If so, how has your mentor helped you with your career? Those of us who have been fortunate enough to have a mentor know how valuable the relationship is and the advantages that it has offered us. Before we continue, however, let's define mentoring. Wikipedia offers the following:

> **Mentorship** is a personal developmental relationship in which a more experienced or more knowledgeable person helps to guide a less experienced or less knowledgeable person. However, true mentoring is more than just answering occasional questions or providing ad hoc help. It is about an ongoing relationship of learning, dialogue, and challenge.

Although mentoring has been a part of the professional vernacular for a very long time, its use in organizations has ebbed and flowed. Recently, the use of mentoring has seen a resurgence as the economy has recovered from the Great Recession that began in 2007. There are several reasons for the increased use of mentoring as a means of employee development. Retention of key or high-potential talent is the primary reason. Human resources and business leaders understood that once the economy and hiring improved, key talent would have multiple career options. These leaders, many of whom had mentors themselves, identified mentoring as a retention tool.

Mentoring often occurs in an informal way. The relationship is initiated either by a more senior professional who sees that a less-experienced colleague would benefit from his or her mentorship and sees potential in the colleague or by a younger professional who is reaching out to the more senior colleague and asking for his or her mentorship. Either way can work; however, there are a few best practices that set up the relationship for long-term success.

We have often been asked by client organizations to develop structured mentoring programs. These programs are formal versions of mentoring with specific objectives for specific employee organizations. Before developing the program itself, it is important that you begin by articulating the business case for mentoring in your organization. The following outlines the benefits of and business case for a mentoring program.

Make Your Case

You want to identify the key reasons for mentoring employees early in their careers. Consider the following points when making the business case for creating a mentoring program in your organization:

- *Reduces turnover and recruiting costs.* Mentoring relationships can help retain talented people because they give these people a stronger commitment to the organization.

- *Helps employees to feel supported.* Talented people are much less likely to leave if they feel that they are supported in their work and are made aware, for example, of new opportunities that their mentor suggests.

- *Helps employees early in their career learn skills and gain knowledge.* Mentoring is an excellent example of informal learning, which is the way people learn 80 percent of the time in the business world.

- *Assists in career growth, building leadership capacity, and increasing bench strength.* Mentees can put their learning on a fast track with mentoring. If they're headed toward management, for example, the mentoring may focus on becoming a better leader and manager.

- *Keeps employees on board.* Both mentees and mentors are about 20 percent less likely to leave the organization than nonmentoring employees.

- *Helps salaries increase.* Both mentees and mentors are about 20 percent more likely than nonmentoring employees to experience a change in salary grade.

Benefits for Mentors

- *Enhances professional growth.* Mentors hone their coaching, leadership, and communication skills as they advise their mentees, and they can, in turn, apply these skills to their own day-to-day work.

- *Increases knowledge and insights about other employees.* Mentoring allows mentors to work with employees of different ages, backgrounds, values, styles of working, and levels of professional expertise. Mentors increase their employee network at different levels and know more about what's going on in the organization.

- *Aids with introspection.* Mentors often find that they gain new insight into their job and how they are performing. When mentees ask why a mentor does things a certain way, it often causes the mentor to reexamine his or her advice, take a critical look at how he or she functions as a leader, and explore what areas he or she may need to adjust for improvement.

- *Helps others grow in their profession.* Mentors gain the satisfaction of sharing their experiences with others and take pleasure in seeing the results of their work.

Benefits for Mentees

- *Gains inside advice from experienced and successful employees.* Mentees who have specific goals that they want to achieve in their work can garner meaningful insights from mentors who have vast knowledge and years of experience to share.

- *Gets insider perspectives* into the best ways to improve their skills, navigate their career, and network within the organization.

- *Receives encouragement and challenges* to achieve new goals and explore new areas of their careers.

- *Learns about the organization's dos and don'ts.*

Roles and Responsibilities

Now that you have made the business case, it is critical that you outline and communicate the role that each participant in the mentoring process is responsible for carrying out.

Mentor Role and Responsibilities

- Commit to and actively build a relationship with your mentee.

- Create an open and trusting environment.

- Be prepared for each interaction with your mentee.

- Share your career and learning experiences that will support your mentee's growth and development.

Mentee Role and Responsibilities

- Commit to building a relationship with your mentor.

- Prepare for each interaction.

- Complete any assignments that your mentor suggests.

- Integrate learnings from your mentor into your performance and development.

Human Resources Role and Responsibilities

- Maintain ownership and facilitation of the mentor program.

- Provide guidance to both mentors and mentees as needed.

- Provide program participants with tools and resources that support their success.

- Collect and analyze program data to determine both the impact of the program and opportunities for improvement.

Training Camp for Mentors

By clearly outlining the roles and responsibilities of your mentor program, you set up each participant for success. The next phase of program development is to train each participant prior to launching your program. The training phase can be done in several different ways. It is important that you think through the best way to reach your participant audiences and the best means by which to engage them in the training.

Before you design your training, it is important that you assess the competency of your mentor population against a *mentor success profile*. A successful mentor:

- Is highly self-aware.

- Works to understand others.

- Uses key communication skills:

  - Actively listens.

  - Asks effective questions.

  - Gives feedback.

These skills and behaviors are critical to creating and sustaining a strong mentoring relationship. Mentor training should include a module on each of these skills; however, how each module is presented in the training needs to take the current skill level of your audience into account. Make the training fun and interactive and your mentors will be more likely to be engaged in it and retain the key learnings offered.

Practice Active Listening

Most of us believe that we are good listeners—and most of us are wrong! As noted in the mentor success profile, active listening is a core skill for creating the right environment for an effective mentor-mentee relationship. Table 8.1 is an assessment tool that will help your mentors evaluate how well they listen and what they need to work on.

Table 8.1 **Mentor Assessment Tool**			
While Someone Is Talking, I:	**Usually**	**Sometimes**	**Rarely**
Plan how I'm going to respond	1	3	5
Maintain eye contact with the speaker	5	3	1
Take notes as appropriate	5	3	1
Notice the feeling behind the words	5	3	1 *(continues)*

Table 8.1 **Mentor Assessment Tool** (continued)			
While Someone Is Talking, I:	**Usually**	**Sometimes**	**Rarely**
Find myself thinking about other things while the person is talking	1	3	5
Watch for body language	5	3	1
Interrupt the speaker to make a point	5	3	1
Am distracted by other demands on my time	1	3	5
Listen for the message without immediately judging or evaluating it	1	3	1
Ask questions to get more information and encourage the speaker to continue	5	3	1
Repeat in my own words what I've just heard to ensure that I understand	5	3	1

Scale:

44–60: You are an active listener.

28–43: You are a good listener with room for improvement.

12–27: You need to focus on improving your listening skills.

Mentor, Know Thyself

In our work with mentor programs, we have found that it was highly beneficial for mentees and mentors to reflect on themselves before entering into the relationship. To help them do this, we created a profile template (see Table 8.2) for the mentor role and ask each mentor to complete the profile and share it with his or her mentee prior to their first meeting.

Table 8.2 **Build a Profile**
Step 1: Complete the first part of the profile and share it with your mentee.

Choose the Statements That Best Describe You

- ❏ Talk things through
- ❏ Think things through
- ❏ Prefer to communicate via e-mail
- ❏ Prefer to communicate face-to-face or Skype

- ❏ Focus on immediate issues and what works now
- ❏ Focus on the future and the long-term impact
- ❏ Start with facts and build to the big picture
- ❏ Start with the big picture and build to facts

- ❏ List the factual pros and cons of a situation
- ❏ Use logic to make a decision
- ❏ Understand how the decision will affect others
- ❏ Understand how others feel before making a decision

- ❏ Create a project plan and follow it
- ❏ Create an outline and use it as a guide
- ❏ Meet deadlines or come in early
- ❏ Work up to deadlines

Step 2: Complete the second part of the profile and share it with your mentee. You may share this part of the profile in the first or second discussion with your mentee.

	I Prefer To	Notes
Communication style		
Problem solving		
Decision making		
Work style		

Getting to Know Your Mentee

To build a strong relationship with a mentee and to understand how to best support his or her development, it is important for the mentor to observe his or her mentee and build a profile over time by identifying the behaviors and characteristics outlined in the following checklist.

How Does Your Mentee Communicate?

- Does he or she talk things through with you or with others?

- Does he or she think things through and then ask questions?

- Does he or she come to your work area, call you, text, Skype, or send e-mails?

- Does he or she create or ask for an agenda for your meetings and conversations?

- What type of questions does he or she ask you?

- Does he or she start with detailed or big-picture questions?

- Does he or she ask questions that pertain to current issues or challenges?

- Does he or she ask more questions about long-term or future situations?

- Does he or she tend to jump from one subject to another?

- Does he or she tend to address things "in order"?

- Does he or she have a need to finalize or finish topics, or does he or she leave things more open-ended?

How Does Your Mentee Make Decisions?

- Does he or she use a pros and cons approach?

- Does he or she start with the effect on him- or herself or the effect on others?

- Does he or she start with the facts of the situation?

- Is he or she influenced by how they feel about an issue before making a decision?

What Type of Work Style Does Your Mentee Have?

- Is his or her work area well organized?

- Does he or she tend to work out of piles?

- Does he or she need to have structure?

- Does he or she prefer to go with the flow?

- Is it important for him or her to finish one project or task before moving on to another?

- Does he or she tend to have several topics, tasks, and projects going at a time?

The responses to these questions enable the mentor to build his or her mentee's profile. Use the chart in Table 8.3 to record your findings.

First Impressions Count

The first meeting between the mentor and the mentee sets the stage for the entire relationship. To make that first meeting a success, it is critical for the mentor to outline a plan and be prepared. Four components of the plan for mentors are as follows:

Table 8.3 **Mentee Profile**		
Name		**Notes**
Role		
Career interests:		
Challenges		
Strengths		
Prefers to:		
Communication style		
Problem solving		
Decision making		
Work style		

1. Preparation

- Complete and review the mentor profile.

- Create a meeting agenda.

- Choose a setting for the meeting.

2. Content

- Take time to get to know each other.

- Discuss logistics.

- Discuss confidentiality.

- Set initial objectives (discuss topics).

- Review and sign agreement (if applicable).

3. Summary and next steps

- Review key points.

- Clearly identify any action items.

- Set up the next meeting or call.

4. Debrief and follow up

- Assess the meeting dynamics.

- Update the mentee profile based on interaction.

- Make notes for improvement.

Make It Official

Some organizations find that it is effective to include a formal contract between the mentor and the mentee. Here is an overview of such a contract.

Purpose

- To formally articulate the purpose and focus of the relationship

- To outline the commitments made by both participants:

    - Calendar of meetings

    - Confidentiality

    - Active participation

    - Open and honest interaction

A Sample Mentor Agreement

Figure 8.1 gives a sample mentor agreement that you can adapt to your own organizational circumstances.

Figure 8.1 **Sample Mentor Agreement**

This is a development program targeted toward increasing the business knowledge and executive exposure for key talent individuals. Part of this experience will be to work with a senior-level mentor in sessions designed to learn more about our organization and to increase professional development skills.

For our mentoring relationship, I, as the mentor, agree to provide you with support, access to my time for meetings, guidance on specific work-related items, advice, honesty, constructive criticism, and positive feedback. I will also seek feedback from you on how I am meeting your developmental needs.

As a (organization) mentor, I pledge to:

- Make time for our meetings.
- Keep our conversations confidential.
- Focus on you and your development.
- Keep my scheduled meetings with you.
- Limit distractions from e-mails, phone calls, and other such interruptions during our conversations.

I look forward to getting to know you and learning how I can support your future development.

_____   _____

Mentor   Date

You now have the best practices and tools that you need in order to create a customized and effective mentoring program that meets the needs of your organization.

TIPS AND TAKEAWAYS FROM THIS CHAPTER

- A formal mentoring program is an effective retention tool.

- Build the business case for a mentor program based on your organization's needs.

- Clearly outline the roles and responsibilities of each participant in the mentor program.

- Develop customized mentor training that focuses on the skills included in the mentor success profile.

- Provide your mentors and mentees with the resources they need in order to be successful.

CHAPTER 9

Locker Essentials

How do you know which skills employees and leaders should focus on developing? In earlier chapters, we outlined the importance of making development relevant to and consistent with the organization's culture. We have also shared best-practice roles and responsibilities in the assessment and development processes. In this chapter, we will provide a framework for using some tools that have long been considered essentials in the learning and development profession, including multirater or 360-degree feedback, feed*forward*, and on-the-job and stretch assignments in your assessment and development strategies.

Over the past 20 years, learning and development professionals have recognized the positive effect of a *blended learning* approach to development. As the name suggests, blended learning is the use of a combination of learning and development techniques and tools to allow employees to learn a new concept, skill, or behavior; apply what they learned; and get feedback on how well they applied what they learned and what they still need to work on. Figure 9.1 depicts the many facets of blended learning.

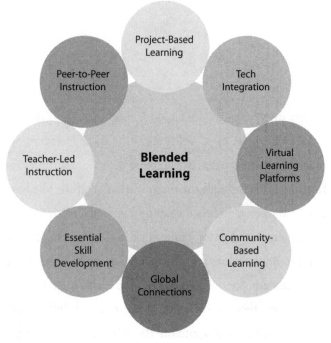

Figure 9.1 **Blended Learning**

As Figure 9.1 illustrates, there are a number of options within a blended learning model. Of course, not all the options are used in any one development plan or strategy. Typically the human resources partner will identify which options to use given the development opportunity.

Aim Before You Shoot

Prior to identifying the strategy to be used, you need to determine what needs to be developed. The multirater or "360-degree feedback" tool is a proven method for identifying the skills and/or behaviors that an employee needs to either further leverage or improve. There are thousands of different 360-degree feedback products on the market, most of which are designed on a classic multirater platform.

We went to Wikipedia again to get a commonly applied definition.

> In human resources or industrial psychology, **360-degree feedback**, also known as **multi-rater feedback**, **multi source feedback**, or **multi source assessment**, is feedback that comes from members of an employee's immediate work circle. Most often, 360-degree feedback will include direct feedback from an employee's subordinates, peers, and supervisor(s), as well as a self-evaluation. It can also include, in some cases, feedback from external sources,

such as customers and suppliers or other interested stakeholders.

People who are receiving feedback to enable them to plan and map specific paths in their development often use the results from a 360-degree evaluation.

Once you decide that 360-degree feedback is a valuable method for assessing skills and behaviors, you need to determine what skills and behaviors will be assessed. In other words, on what skills will employees receive feedback? Many organizations initiate a project to identify core competencies for employees and leaders in the organization. Others identify a success profile for key or specific positions and include the success profile skills in the 360-degree tool. As mentioned earlier in this chapter, there are many 360-degree products in the marketplace that offer research-based competency models for all levels, from individual contributors to executive leaders. These products provide a menu of competencies from which you can build customized success profiles.

Kicking It Off

Figure 9.2 outlines a best-practice 360-degree feedback process.

360 Development Process

Project and Communication Planning

Purpose: To clearly articulate the project and communication plan and their implementation
- Discuss key objectives with the CEO and HR
- Confirm success profile using our competency model and recommended success profile
- Prepare for team communication

Kickoff

Purpose: Initiate the process
- Do this during a team meeting and in memo form
- Provide the team with an overview of the process
- Outline roles and responsibilities

360-Degree Process

Purpose: Implement the multirater process (2–3 weeks)
- Each team member will choose up to 10 raters
- Communicate the process and role to raters
- Distribute survey tools via e-mail
- Raters complete survey and submit to processing center
- Completed reports sent to facilitators

Analysis of Feedback

Purpose: To have a thorough understanding of each team member's report and to be prepared to facilitate a discussion with him or her about the feedback data
- Review report in detail
- Identify key data points against success profile
- Prepare for discussion

Individual Feedback Session

Purpose: Provide each team member with an analysis of his or her feedback data and a starting point for his or her development plan (1.5–2 hours each)
- Walk each team member through each part of the feedback report, providing perspective
- Prepare him or her to begin to focus on areas of strength and development

Development Plan

Purpose: To coach each team member in creating an individual development plan and coaching to support the plan (2 meetings for each leader)
- Review a draft plan created by the team member
- Coach team member in reviewing the draft with his or her manager
- Coach each team member on finalizing and implementing his or her plan
- Provide regular updates and coaching to both the CEO and HR

Figure 9.2 **360-Degree Feedback Process**

Before the 360-degree feedback survey invitations are sent to the survey participants, the individual who is asking for feedback should communicate personally with each of them. This ensures that everyone understands his or her role and increases the commitment level. Figure 9.3 is a template for an e-mail communication that you can customize.

Figure 9.3 **360-Degree Leadership Feedback Survey Introductory E-mail Template**

As part of the leadership coaching process that I am participating in at (insert your organization's name here), I will be asking you for your feedback on certain leadership competencies to identify those in which I am successful and those in which I have opportunity for improvement.

In the next few days, you will be receiving an e-mail from (name the 360-degree provider here) containing a link to an online feedback survey, (insert survey name here). Your feedback is important to me, and I want to thank you in advance for making this investment in my success.

I am working with an external coach, (insert coach's name here), to interpret my feedback and create a development plan. All of your responses will be confidential.

Please be frank about my performance at (insert your orga-nization's name here) in both your numeric scores and your comments, as that information will help me serve you, and the organization, more effectively.

Please contact me with any questions you might have.

Thank you.

Ready to Launch

Figures 9.4 and 9.5 are samples of a 360-degree feedback questionnaire and a 360-degree feedback report.

Figure 9.4 **360-Degree Feedback Questionnaire**

This multisource feedback instrument was designed for XYZ Corporation by Human Resources Consulting.

You are assessing: Pamela Jones, supervisor

This questionnaire was designed especially for XYZ Corporation to provide Pamela Jones with 360-degree feedback. Its purpose, in the context of a changing work world, is to assist Pamela in developing her capabilities fully.

(continues)

In order to provide Pamela with the broadest possible perspective, feedback is being requested from a range of people. You have been selected because you are familiar with how she works.

Please Be Frank

In order to be most helpful to Pamela, please answer the questions that follow in a completely candid manner, without being unduly critical or uncritical.

Your Individual Reply Is Confidential

People sometimes wonder whether their reply will be seen by the person who is being assessed or by other people in the organization. In fact, all replies are held in strictest confidence.

Your answers will be averaged with those of others in a report that will provide a comprehensive but anonymous picture of how Pamela is seen in the workplace.

How to Respond

This questionnaire allows you to provide two types of feedback.

1. Replying to Numerical Questions

Please indicate the extent to which you agree or disagree that the following statements apply to Pamela Jones.

Your choice of responses ranges from 1 (which means that you strongly disagree) to 10 (which means that you strongly agree). Please select any of the numbers from 1 to 10 so as to provide a fine-tuned response to each statement.

Simply click on the circle that corresponds with your selection.

2. Providing Comments

At the end of each section, you will find space for unstructured comments.

Please consider these guidelines to make your comments most helpful:

- What do you appreciate about Pamela's work style?

- What are the key challenges that you believe she should focus on?

- What suggestions do you have about how she should do so?

Numerical Questions About Pamela Jones

Business Skills and Experience

1. Understands the business requirements and financial policies of the organization.   *(continues)*

Not Enough Info		Strongly Disagree				Disagree		Agree		Strongly Agree
N	1	2	3	4	5	6	7	8	9	10

2. Formulates strategic goals and objectives.

Not Enough Info		Strongly Disagree				Disagree		Agree		Strongly Agree
N	1	2	3	4	5	6	7	8	9	10

3. Is proactive, responding to opportunities, solving problems, and planning for action.

Not Enough Info		Strongly Disagree				Disagree		Agree		Strongly Agree
N	1	2	3	4	5	6	7	8	9	10

4. Makes wise tactical decisions and sticks with them.

Not Enough Info		Strongly Disagree				Disagree		Agree		Strongly Agree
N	1	2	3	4	5	6	7	8	9	10

5. Your comments regarding Business Skills and Experience:

Professional and Technical Skills

6. Stays on top of developments in her field.

Not Enough Info		Strongly Disagree				Disagree		Agree		Strongly Agree
N	1	2	3	4	5	6	7	8	9	10

7. Pursues innovative opportunities to provide new services.

Not Enough Info	Strongly Disagree		Disagree		Agree		Strongly Agree	
N	1	2	3	4	5	6	7	8	9	10

8. Anticipates problems and plans effective solutions.

Not Enough Info	Strongly Disagree		Disagree		Agree		Strongly Agree	
N	1	2	3	4	5	6	7	8	9	10

9. Your comments regarding Professional and Technical Skills:

Questionnaire Conclusion

The section you have just completed may not convey everything you would like to say about Pamela Jones. The comments section here allows you to add supplementary information that you wish to express. Your contribution is valuable.

Consider these guidelines:

Please think about Pamela Jones's overall contribution to the workplace. Add any suggestions that would help her maintain her strengths and improve her skills.

Comments:

Thank you for taking the time to complete this questionnaire, which will provide Pamela Jones with valuable assistance.

360° Feedback Report—Competency Items

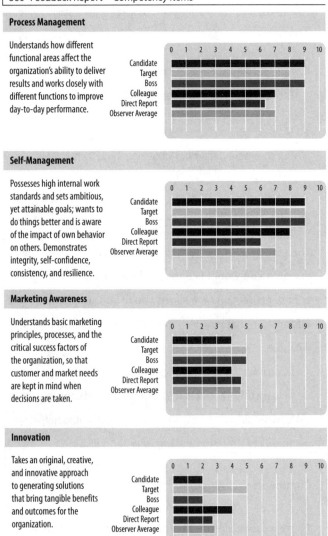

Process Management

Understands how different functional areas affect the organization's ability to deliver results and works closely with different functions to improve day-to-day performance.

Self-Management

Possesses high internal work standards and sets ambitious, yet attainable goals; wants to do things better and is aware of the impact of own behavior on others. Demonstrates integrity, self-confidence, consistency, and resilience.

Marketing Awareness

Understands basic marketing principles, processes, and the critical success factors of the organization, so that customer and market needs are kept in mind when decisions are taken.

Innovation

Takes an original, creative, and innovative approach to generating solutions that bring tangible benefits and outcomes for the organization.

Figure 9.5   **Sample 360-Degree Feedback Report**

As these figures illustrate, a 360-degree feedback survey and report provide employees with a quantitative and qualitative view of how their stakeholders perceive their ability to demonstrate specific skills.

Now that you have the 360-degree data, what do you do with them? It is critical that 360-degree feedback be carefully managed. Your organization's 360-degree protocols should include the following components:

1. The purpose of 360-degree surveys

2. Employee populations who are eligible to participate in the 360-degree process

3. Roles and responsibilities:

   • Human Resources

   • Employee

   • Manager

   • Third party, if applicable

4. Who will receive a copy of the 360-degree report

5. How the reports will be distributed and maintained

Once these questions have been answered, it is important to communicate them clearly to the organization's leadership and implement the protocols in a consistent way. Organizations that have not managed their 360-degree process with integrity have essentially eliminated that process as an effective development tool.

Turn Feedback on Its Head

Marshall Goldsmith, a globally recognized leadership thought leader and executive coach, challenged leaders to integrate feed*forward* into their ongoing development efforts. The purpose of the Marshall Goldsmith Feed*Forward* Tool is to provide individuals, teams, and organizations with suggestions for the future and to help them achieve a positive change in their behavior.

We have introduced the feed*forward* concept in leadership development workshops. Here's how it works.

The exercise typically lasts for 10 to 15 minutes, and the average participant has six or seven dialogue sessions. In the exercise, participants are asked to:

- Pick one behavior that they would like to change. Change in this behavior should make a significant positive difference in their lives.

- Describe this behavior to randomly selected fellow participants. This is done in one-on-one dialogues. It can be done quite simply by saying something like, "I want to be a better listener."

- Ask for feed*forward*—for two suggestions for the future that might help them achieve a positive change in their selected behavior. If participants have worked together in the past, they are not allowed to give *any* feedback about the past. They are allowed to give only ideas for the future.

- Listen attentively to the suggestions and take notes. Participants are not allowed to comment on the suggestions in any way. They are not allowed to critique the suggestions or even to make positive judgmental statements, such as, "That's a good idea."

- Thank the other participant in the dialogue for his or her suggestions.

- Ask the other person what he or she would like to change.

- Provide feed*forward*—two suggestions aimed at helping the other person change.   *(continues)*

- Say, "You are welcome," when you are thanked for your suggestions. The entire process of both giving and receiving feed*forward* usually takes about two minutes.

- Find another participant and repeat the process. Continue doing this until the exercise is stopped.

  When the exercise is finished, ask participants to provide one word that best describes their reaction to this experience. Ask them to complete the sentence, "This exercise was. . . ." The words provided are almost always extremely positive, such as *great, energizing, useful,* or *helpful.* The word that is most commonly mentioned is *fun!*

Try introducing feed*forward* into your development program; it is a fun and effective way for your employees to make changes in how they interact with others.

Get Out There!

Most of us are aware of the statistic that 70 percent of employee development happens on the job, not in classroom-based training. However, many learning and development professionals struggle to design more practical learning opportunities that can be consistently applied. As we discussed at the beginning of this chapter, a blended learning approach has been shown to be more effective than one-dimensional methods.

The following case studies will illustrate how to structure on-the-job development successfully.

CASE STUDY

Employee: Paul

Position: Director of operations

Development need: Presentation skills. Specifically, Paul needs to improve his ability to present a clear and concise message that is appropriate for his audience.

Importance of skill: Paul is responsible for implementing a new supply chain strategy. Part of his responsibility is to present the business case for the new strategy to upper management and to his team.

(continues)

Development Strategies

1. Attend presentation skills program:

   - Understand the core components, skills, and techniques required for presenting effectively.

2. Apply the skills and techniques learned in the program.

   - Identify on-the-job opportunities for practicing and applying the skills learned.

On-the-Job Opportunities

- Paul is scheduled to present the business case for the new supply chain strategy to senior leadership at its weekly meeting. Paul is on the agenda for 20 minutes. The purpose of the presentation is for Paul to inform the audience. In addition, Paul needs to be prepared to respond to questions from the audience.

Application

- Paul's manager and coach (internal or external) will work closely with him to outline how he can apply the skills learned in his training to the specific presentation just described.

- Paul's presentation content and delivery should reflect that he understood his development opportunities and used the knowledge he gained from his training and his coach to address them.

- Paul should solicit feedback from a trusted colleague who attended the senior leadership meeting and apply that feedback to his continued development.

CASE STUDY

Employee: Sarah

Position: Project manager

Development need: Decision making. Sarah is a high-potential employee. She has managed complex projects and found creative solutions to challenges. However, because of her need to analyze each possible solution, she has missed deadlines

(continues)

on two key projects. Sarah needs to develop the ability to make a decision without having all the information.

Development Strategies

- Provide Sarah with a peer coach who has experience in project management and has consistently demonstrated the ability to make decisions based on the information available.

- Clearly outline the purpose, roles, and responsibilities of the peer coaching relationship to both Sarah and her coach.

- Identify a current or upcoming project that Sarah and her peer coach can work on together so that Sarah can see live examples of how her peer coach manages situations in which a timely decision is needed, but only limited information is available.

- Engage Sarah's manager in the development process. It is important that she create an environment that rewards and recognizes Sarah's efforts to make timely decisions, as well as a tolerance for measured risk.

The number of on-the-job opportunities is endless; however, many managers miss them. By training leaders to understand the value of leveraging real work as development opportunities, you will significantly increase the number of developmental opportunities that are available to employees.

TIPS AND TAKEAWAYS FROM THIS CHAPTER

- Understand the benefits of blended learning development.

- Incorporate 360-degree feedback into your assessment and development strategy.

- Try feed*forward*.

- Leverage on-the-job development opportunities.

What's Next?

Our objective in writing this book was to provide you with an easy-to-use, go-to resource that supports the assessment and development work that is being conducted in your organization. Employee development has become more complex and more interesting over the past 10 years and will continue to evolve as the next generations come onto the scene. To keep up with these dynamics, HR professionals and other leaders have a responsibility to understand how to best reach, motivate, nurture, and support their team members while holding them accountable for meeting performance expectations. The only way to accomplish this is to understand their role and responsibility, then create a plan and carry that plan through.

The strategies, tools, and checklists in this tool kit will assist you in both creating and implementing your assessment and development plan. Follow these steps to make it all come together:

1. *Identify your objectives.* What do you want to accomplish?

2. *Build your business case to support your objectives.* What organizational challenge or issue will your objectives address and add value to? Outline the return on investment.

3. *Identify the right partners.* Who are the right people in your organization to support and drive your objectives?

4. *Keep track of and leverage your successes.* How will you measure your success?

5. *Get feedback.* How will you know whether you are hitting or missing the mark?

6. *Share your success.* How will you let others know about your wins?

Integrating the tools and strategies contained in these pages into these six steps will put you on the path to providing each specific audience within your organization with development opportunities that position it for long-term success. The journey has just begun, and we thank you for taking us along with you!

Questions and Answers

No question is unimportant, so if you don't know something and you need or want to know it, ask. Over the course of Anne and Brenda's professional careers, they have worked with human resources leaders, as well as other leaders across the organization, who have questions about what professional and/or career development is and how they can engage in a development program or general opportunity. Here is a set of questions that we have been asked and our corresponding responses.

1. I have been in my role for three years, and I am looking to move to the next level. Would participating in a leadership development program benefit me?

   Response: First, participating in a leadership development program does not ensure that you will be promoted. However, continuous development is a great habit to establish early in your career and one that will serve you well. Anne calls this "upgrading" yourself. Second, do your research and gain an understanding of what your organization's leadership development program offers and how that fits with your development needs? Talk with your boss, a human resources partner, employee development coach, and others who may help you understand both what the program has to offer and what you need if you are to bridge the gap between your current skill and performance level and what the next step requires.

2. My boss has asked me to leave my current role and take over a project that has missed deadlines and is over budget. He believes that this is a stretch assignment that will further my career. Should I be excited or concerned?

   Response: Generally speaking, a turnaround assignment can be a terrific developmental opportunity. To set yourself up for success, remember these three rules:

   • Align with the project owner and the sponsor concerning deliverables and expectations.

   • Understand the project stakeholders and their position and influence.

   • Determine and negotiate the resources you need.

3. I am the new leader of an established team, and my initial observations tell me that three of the five team members are solid, one is a high performer, and I am not able to connect with the fifth. I am not sure how to manage these different levels of performance and engagement. Where do I start?

Response: The first step is to use a framework or structure to capture the current state of your team. Second, clearly define the competencies and performance that the organization needs from your team. Then you are ready to work with the team members individually to "meet them where they are" and outline a development strategy and plan. This may include 360-degree feedback, participation in development programs, one-on-one coaching, and on-the-job development assignments. Remember, you are a key partner in your team's development, which requires dedicated time and actionable and regular feedback.

4. I am a human resources business partner supporting our shared services functions. Although our senior leadership includes talent development as an important core value, there is little investment in or importance given to development. The leaders I support are asking for my help; how can I provide what they need without broader backing?

Response: Although this can be challenging, there are several development strategies that you can leverage that will have a significant impact. Examples include:

- Build a business case for investment in development initiatives. Gather facts that demonstrate the negative impact of little or no investment in development. For example, it can lead to high turnover of key talent and a lack of a talent bench. Then articulate how a talent development strategy would address this business issue.

- Hold regular development discussions with the senior leaders within your client groups. Provide them with guidance and tools (use those included in this book) that will increase their ability to coach and develop their team members.

- Keep yourself up to date on relevant leadership development concepts and applications to share with your leaders.

- Develop a speaker or a lunch-and-learn series with local or internal experts.

- Establish a leadership/business book club.

These strategies are high gain and low cost. Tap into your professional network for additional ideas that will help you fill the void.

5. My boss has asked me to participate in a 360-degree feedback process. Should I look for a new job?

Response: Generally speaking, being asked to participate in a 360-degree feedback process should be viewed as a positive sign; it shows that your boss and your organization are willing to invest in your development. If you are concerned, you may want to share your concern with your boss, your human resources partner, or any colleagues who have previously participated in a 360-degree process at your company. Use this experience to learn how others perceive you and be open to their feedback.

Strategic Thinking

Developing strategic thinking is a common development need for employees who are making the transition from an individual contributor role to a higher-level and more complex role. The following process is effective at helping these employees understand how to strengthen their ability to think more strategically.

Curiosity Can Lead to Strategic Thinking

Senior leaders value employees who are proven operators *and* who are capable of looking at the bigger picture and providing help in developing the way forward for the business.

Your ability to cultivate both sets of skills will help you strengthen your professional value proposition and help to differentiate you from your peers. This differentiation might just be the meaningful issue for that next promotion.

Much of strategic thinking is about knowing the right questions to ask and then seeking answers to these questions. Jack Welch, the former chairman and CEO of GE, famously said:

> In real life, strategy is actually very straightforward. You pick a general direction and implement like hell.

While there's some comfort in the pure, raw simplicity of that thought, what Welch *didn't* share in this quote is that he subjected his managers and business unit leaders to 40 or so incredibly challenging (to answer) questions as part of the process of picking that direction and building the implementation plan.

The opportunity for all of us, from senior executives to frontline professionals, is to blend some of Welch's simplicity on this often confusing topic of strategy with the ongoing pursuit of answers to some critical questions.

Six Question Sets to Help Jump-Start Your Strategic Curiosity

1. *Our business situation.* How do we make money to-day? What do our customers truly pay for? Why do they choose us over our competitors? How are we meaningfully different from our competitors?

2. *Our changing world.* What's changing and what's changed in our world that will affect us? Our customers? Our competitors? Our partners? What are we doing to leverage or exploit those changes?

3. *Our customers.* What do we know about our customers and their challenges that we can acquire and apply expertise to help solve? Can we do this to our advantage and to the disadvantage of our competitors?

4. *Our ecosystem.* How does our business fit within the ecosystem of players that serve our target customers? Are there opportunities for us to do more or less to improve our differentiation and our profitability? Can we partner or acquire to do something that will help us differentiate ourselves and add value for our customers?

5. *Our opportunities to change the rules.* What can we do to change the game for our competitors? What might our competitors do to change the game for us? What's our counter?

6. *What to do and what not to do.* How do we choose what to do and, more important, what not to do? What filters are we using for our decision making? How can we improve or clarify those filters?

The Bottom Line for Now

While that's a fairly hefty set of questions (to answer), we view them as simply thought starters. No one function or level in the organization owns those questions, although senior executives are responsible for ensuring that they are answered and acted upon.

Strategy and strategic thinking and experimentation should not be left just to senior executives and well-heeled consultants. The work of strategy and building the future is everyone's business. Effective senior managers value strategic thinking (and actions) in their employees, and your willingness to ask and seek answers to these critical issues is an indicator that you may be ready for more responsibility.

Appendix

The following templates are included to augment your assessment and coaching strategies. Make them your own and see the results!

Coaching Session Agenda Template

Use the following template to plan for a coaching meeting.

Coaching Session Agenda Template	
Purpose	• Part of the (function or team name) leadership development process • Allow each individual to focus on his or her specific development needs • Provide each team member with one-on-one direction related to improving skills and behaviors that will lead to continued success
Development discussion	• Review the feedback report • Discuss the feedback report in a midyear performance discussion meeting with the manager • Development areas to focus on • Strength(s) to leverage *(continues)*

Coaching Session Agenda Template *(continued)*	
Development plan	• Review the plan • Begin to draft the plan • Assign next steps for the plan • Provide on-the-job opportunities to practice
Next steps	• Agree to a calendar of meetings • Arrange development assignments

Ask for Clarifying Feedback Tool

Make the most of the feedback you have received from your 360-degree process by following these steps. Gathering clarifying feedback will allow you to have a clear understanding of the areas you need to develop, as well as your strengths.

Asking for Clarifying Feedback	
Overview	An important step in your leadership development process is to clearly understand the feedback that you received from your rater groups. The feedback that you receive in your 360-degree report often brings more questions than answers. To fill in the gaps, it is important for you to gather clarifying feedback from appropriate "representatives" within your rater group(s).

Asking for Clarifying Feedback *(continued)*	
Sources	• Bosses are generally good sources for giving you a perspective on how peers may perceive you, as well as on your task planning, selling up, and problem-solving skills. • Direct reports are generally good sources for feedback on your day-to-day behavior, social skills, and team building ability. • Peers are generally good sources for feedback on your persuasion, negotiation, listening, and common cause skills.
Be realistic	Many people are reluctant to give people the same feedback face-to-face that they put into a confidential report. They will almost always be more positive face-to-face. To best understand them and to demonstrate that you are serious about your development, say this: "You are doing me a favor. I need your help to better understand my feedback and take action."

Pave the way	Make statements initially rather than asking questions; for example:
	    "I would appreciate your input on the following:
	    "I think I may focus too much on my customers and not enough on my direct reports.
	    "My feedback indicates that the people around me feel that I do not do well with conflict situations.
	    "An area that I clearly need to work on is my ability to listen effectively."

Summary	It is easier for most people to reply to statements rather than questions, which may put them on the spot. It is important that you accept whatever the replies are. You can ask questions to clarify and summarize what people say, but never counter the feedback or you'll probably get no more in the future.

Active Listening

Use this template to do a self-review of how your active listening presentation discussion went.

Active Listening Template
Work Situation

Practice conversation:
 	
    Who was the conversation with?
 	
    What was the topic?
 	
    What was the outcome of the conversation?

What active listening techniques did you use (for example, taking notes, paraphrasing, eye contact, or reflecting)?	
Give us a couple of examples of questions that you asked to ensure understanding.	
How did the person respond?	
What could you have done differently?	

Getting Feedback on Your Conversation Ask the following questions of the person you had the discussion with.	
How well did you feel I listened to you?	
What were some of the things I did that made you feel like I was listening?	
What could I have done better to show you that I was listening?	

Active Listening Template *(continued)*	
Personal Situation	

Practice conversation:
 	
    Who was the conversation with?
 	
    What was the topic?
 	
    What was the outcome of the conversation?	

What active listening techniques did you use (for example, taking notes, paraphrasing, eye contact, or reflecting)?	
Give us a couple of examples of questions that you asked to ensure understanding.	
How did the person respond?	
What could you have done differently?	
Getting Feedback on Your Conversation Ask the following questions of the person you had the discussion with.	
How well did you feel I listened to you?	
What were some of the things I did that made you feel like I was listening?	
What could I have done better to show you that I was listening?	

Notes

Chapter 1

1. See www.mckinsey.com for more information.
2. Ed Michaels, Helen Handfield-Jones, and Beth Axelrod, *The War for Talent* (New York: McKinsey & Co., 2001).

Chapter 2

1. Adam Bryant, *Quick and Nimble: Lessons from Leading CEOs on How to Create a Culture of Innovation* (New York: Times Books, 2014).

Chapter 3

1. David Ulrich, *Human Resources Champions* (Boston: Harvard Business Review Press, 1996).
2. Jason Geller and Arthur H. Mazor, *Global Business Driven HR Transformation: The Journey Continues* (New York: Deloitte Consulting, 2011).
3. Diane Coutu and Carol Kauffman, *What Can Coaches Do for You?* (Boston: Harvard Business Review Press, 2009).

Chapter 4

1. Diane Downey, Tom March, and Adena Berkman, *Assimilating New Leaders: The Key to Executive Retention* (New York: AMACOM, 2001).

2. Michael Watkins, *The First 90 Days: Critical Success Strategies for New Leaders at All Levels* (Boston: Harvard Business School Press, 2003).

3. *Onboarding: The First Line of Engagement* (Boston: Aberdeen Group, 2010).

Index

About the Authors

Brenda Hampel is a founding partner of Connect the Dots Consulting. She leveraged her corporate human resources experience and business acumen to design a consulting model focusing on results that advance both the organization and the person. Brenda is privileged to work with many engaging, smart, and talented executives at dozens of organizations nationwide. She gains a great deal of satisfaction from seeing her clients work through challenging situations successfully, stretching themselves, and finding the right balance with their work.

Brenda's corporate experience includes senior human resources positions at Lennox Industries, Bath & Body Works, and Cardinal Health. Brenda and her business partner, Erika Lamont, founded Connect the Dots in 2006 to focus their expertise in executive coaching, team dynamics, and onboarding. Brenda, Erika, and their team of consultants are fortunate to partner with progressive and dynamic leaders and organizations such as Volkswagen Group of America, Audi of America, Lane Bryant, Tween Brands, TJX Companies, and The Ohio State University and Medical Center.

Brenda is the co-author of two additional books, *Solving Employee Performance Problems* (McGraw-Hill) and *Perfect Phrases for New Employee Orientation and Onboarding* (McGraw-Hill). Brenda has presented at numerous human resources conferences and keeps abreast of current leadership and human resources issues and practices by actively contributing to professional online and printed sources.

In addition to her professional endeavors, Brenda enjoys spending time outdoors, exercising, and exploring new places and adventures with her husband, Jeff. She also loves spending time with her two daughters, Alexandria and Jordan, and supporting them as they launch their own exciting careers and lives.

Brenda would love to hear from readers and can be reached through her website at: www.connectthedots consulting.com; her direct email is: bhampel@connectthe dotsconsulting.com, and her direct dial is: 614.793.8836.

Anne Bruce knows how to acknowledge, evaluate, attract, nurture, and develop top talent! Her popular keynote speech and seminar workshop, "America's Got Talent in the Workplace and It Comes from All Over the World," has received rave reviews from Dallas to Dubai. Anne is a bestselling author with 20 books published to date, including *Discover True North: A Four-Week Approach to Ignite Your Passion and Activate Your Potential* (McGraw-Hill), *Be Your Own Mentor* (McGraw-Hill), *Building a High-Morale Workplace* (McGraw-Hill), *The Manager's Guide to Motivating Employees* (McGraw-Hill), *Solving Employee Performance Problems* (McGraw-Hill), *Perfect Phrases for Documenting Employee Performance Problems* (McGraw-Hill), *Perfect Phrases for Employee Development Plans* (McGraw-Hill), *Mighty Manager Series: How to Motivate Every Employee* (McGraw-Hill), *Leaders Start to Finish: A Roadmap for Developing Top Performers,* 2d ed. (ASTD Press), and *Speak for a Living: The Insider's Guide to Building A Speaking Career* (ASTD Press).

Anne has had the privilege of speaking, writing, and training at prestigious venues and organizations, such as the White House, the Pentagon, Saks Fifth Avenue, Sony International, GEICO, Southwest Airlines, JetBlue, Ben & Jerry's, Baylor University Medical Center, Harvard and

Stanford law schools, MedAmerica Billing Services, Inc. (MBSI), and the Conference Board of Europe.

For details on how to bring this book's training program to your organization, and for information on additional motivational leadership programs, like "The Art of Leadership," "Communications Excellence," "Going from Customer Service Excellence to Customer Service Loyalty," "Performance Coaching for Success," and "Nurturing the Technical Professional," contact Anne at **214-507-8242** or at **Anne@AnneBruce.com**. Please visit her website at www.AnneBruce.com for more information, scheduling press interviews, and fees.